32 Days with Christ's Passion

By Mark R. Etter

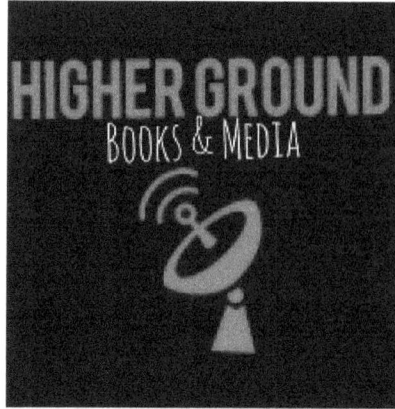

Scripture taken from the HOLY BIBLE, NEW INTERNATIONAL VERSION®. NIV®. Copyright © 1973, 1978, 1984 by International Bible Society. Used by permission of Zondervan. All rights reserved worldwide.

Higher Ground Books & Media
Springfield, Ohio.
http://highergroundbooksandmedia.com

Printed in the United States of America 2018

32 Days with Christ's Passion

By Mark R. Etter

DEDICATION

This book is dedicated to Lou and Carol Noyd who have blessed Bethany Lutheran with their passion for the Lord's ministry.

Table of Contents

32 days series – Grow and Give

Why write another series of devotions? The bible is the key to salvation and a fulfilling life and most Christians know the Bible poorly. This series is built around two ideas – grow and give. The thirty-two devotions cover the passion of Jesus to help you grow stronger in your faith and heal any brokenness that you feel. Each devotion digs deeply into the Bible to help you see and apply the wisdom of scripture to your own life. As you do all 32 devotions, you will see aspects of the cross and resurrection that you may never have seen before. My prayer is that these devotions and the two questions that follow each one will help your faith in the Lord grow greatly so that you can reach your full potential.

Once you have grown, I would challenge you to use the twelve bible studies to give others the joy that you now have. Use the bible studies to share a little of God's love to a friend or a small group so that they may have your joy. The bible studies are reproducible so that you can share them with others with no additional expense. Give the message of these passages to the people that you know who feel broken. Let the people struggling in their faith see the depth of Jesus' love for them. You will find that in giving the lessons away to others that the Lord will help you grow even more in your faith and joy.

Passion Introduction

The passion of Jesus was and is the salvation of mankind. It was so important that he felt He must do the work of the cross. It was so important that He never veered from that purpose. He prepared the disciples for His departure and for the coming of the Holy Spirit that would fulfill His act of salvation as the church was begun. He prepared Himself in the Garden of Eden so that He would not flinch at the sacrifice that He had to make. He took each step foretold in the Old Testament by places like Isaiah 53 with courage and conviction. The salvation of mankind was His obsession. The Bible doesn't hide the pain of Jesus as He completes the plan of salvation or the failure of the disciples as they leave their Lord alone and forsaken at this crucial hour.

These devotions will walk you step by step through the passion. You will sit with Jesus in the upper room as He teaches His disciples about His passion and their place in the kingdom. You will walk with Jesus to Gethsemane and through the trials to hear His prayer and see His resolute obedience to the Father. You will experience His suffering on the cross and learn what His sacrifice means for you. Finally, you will experience the joy of Easter and understand why this is the most important gift you and I receive. Walk with Him through these hours and learn from Him. See His compassion and dedication to you first hand.

As you follow the passion of Jesus, let His passion become your passion. Let your character and values reflect the character of Christ. Let your desire be that others around you might know and believe in this story as you proclaim the love of Jesus and show His influence and blessings in your life. Let others see the care and love that Jesus has for them in a world where it is often each man for himself. We have someone who loves us. You and I know how much Jesus loved us and how He showed that on the cross. It is up to us to help others to see Jesus' passion for their lives and the blessings that are available to every man, woman, and child who believe in Him and His cross.

01 Passion Expressed-Matthew 16:21-23

Context: Our study begins about a year before His crucifixion when Jesus takes the disciples north to Caesarea Philippi so that they can learn what was to come. In the days ahead, He will take them to the mountain where Jesus would be transfigured before them.

The Olympic Games were only a week away. It was what John had prepared for all his life. It was what would define him. Everything in the coming week would be done with an eye to standing on the podium at the swimming competitions next Friday. He would practice till his arms and legs gave out. He would sit with his coach and review his mechanics so that each stroke was smooth and efficient. He would maximize every morsel of food to rebuild muscle and provide energy for that final burst of speed. Swimming had been his life's passion and nothing would be allowed to thwart his success.

Our Lord Jesus Christ had but one passion. He had come into this world to save mankind from their sins. Healing the sick was noble, but the cure was temporary. Teaching would help them understand His ministry and their need, but the crowds never seemed to fully grasp the heart of the gospel. It was the cross that was central for the salvation of mankind. It was at the heart of everything that Jesus did. As the cross drew near, everything Jesus did focused on that passion. His final teaching around the Lord's Supper table and His great prayer in the Garden prepared Him for what was ahead. As we walk with Jesus in these final days, we will see how He single-mindedly went to the cross. It was His passion. It was what He had come to do.

This passion was nothing new. It had been with Jesus from the beginning. He announced that passion to the disciples as He prepared them for the transfiguration and the trip to Jerusalem. "From that time on Jesus began to explain to his disciples that he must go to Jerusalem and suffer many things at the hands of the elders, chief priests, and teachers of the law and that he must be killed and on the third day be raised to life." (v.21) The events of Holy Week were no surprise to Jesus. He knew what was coming and had a passion for fulfilling the plan of redemption through the cross. He wanted salvation for you and for me so much that He would sacrifice Himself willingly. Nothing would be allowed to divert Him from the course that would bring salvation to the world.

Yet, the passion of Jesus was not received well. "Peter took him aside and began to rebuke him. Never, Lord! He said. This shall never happen to you!" (v.22) Peter had just confessed that Jesus was the Messiah (Matthew 16:16). Yet he can't understand how the Messiah could die. Like us, Peter has a vision of triumph and not sacrifice. The trip to Jerusalem should be a trip where the victorious King Jesus claimed God's throne. He cannot understand a picture in which Jesus the Lamb of God marches to His death. Like many after him, Peter did not understand the real price of sin and the triumph that would come in the resurrection. He rejected the sacrifice and focused on the glory of Jesus as a miracle worker and Lord. He didn't understand that a Savior was what the world really needed.

If we are to be useful to the Lord and to appreciate what Jesus did, we need to "have in mind the things of God, (not) the things of men." (v.23) We need to see things as they are and not as we want them to be. In this set of devotions, we want to follow the passion of Jesus and see how He set His eyes on the cross. We want to follow Jesus and understand His sacrifice and His love. We want to watch His movements and His attitudes so that we have the same passion that He has about salvation and about sin. Follow Him and notice that nothing was allowed to get in the way of the cross during that final week. He wanted us to have the victory that would come from His sacrifice. The cross could have been avoided, but Jesus would not let that happen. He wanted to save us from sin more than anything else.

The passion of Jesus is to be our passion. Mankind takes sin too lightly. Mankind doesn't take the penalty for sin seriously. Many around us no longer believe in Jesus or the cross. Follow Jesus and catch His passion for saving mankind. Let His passion encourage you to share the message of the cross with others so that they can be saved as well. Let His passion help you see the price of sin and feel the victory that the cross and the empty tomb bring for us. The passion of Jesus is central to His ministry and to the whole Bible. Jesus knew His mission and would not let anything keep Him from that task. May we catch His passion and His willingness to sacrifice so that others might have this salvation just as we do.

- What is the passion of your life right now? How does your passion affect others around you? How does it relate to the passion of Jesus?

02 Love Stands Out-Mark 14:1-9

Context: Mark seems to put this event after Palm Sunday (Mark 11), while John tells us that it was the Friday before Palm Sunday (John 12:1). Either way, Jesus has come to Jerusalem in preparation for the cross. Mary shows us what it means to love Jesus at a banquet held in Jesus' honor.

The evening news can be depressing as it tells of murder, war, and greed. Evil surrounds our world and makes us feel like evil is winning and the Lord is losing. Can anything change the sad state of our world? The simple answer is yes. Acts of love and kindness change everything. We just have to be daring and bold enough to do them. We have to love because we are loved by Jesus. At times, that may be hard. Surrounded by selfish people, it is easy to become like the crowd. It is easy to withhold our generosity because we feel that we have not been loved. When one person breaks that pattern, it can be powerful. The power of love given in honor to Jesus Christ can fill a room. It is so memorable that it will have an impact for years to come.

It was six days before the Passover (John12:1), that is right before Palm Sunday. Jesus came to stay with Mary and Martha in Bethany and there He received a gift of love. "A woman came with an alabaster jar of very expensive perfume, made of pure nard. She broke the jar and poured the perfume on his head." (v.3) John tells us that this was Mary, the sister of Lazarus (John 12:3). The gift was expensive, worth a full year's salary and its fragrance would have filled the room. Her act of worship showed the depth of love that she had for Jesus. It may be that she was honoring Jesus for raising her brother Lazarus from the dead. Regardless, it is clear that she felt Jesus' love and wanted to honor Him and show Him the depth of her love for Him.

Not everyone understands this gift of love. Unexpectedly, she had poured the valuable perfume on Jesus' head and feet. The other guests were aghast. "Some of those present were saying indignantly to one another, "Why this waste of perfume?" (v.4) Many felt that if she had wanted to worship God, she should have sold the perfume and given the proceeds to the poor. Not understanding what she has done, the others rebuke her for this gift of love. John tells us that it is Judas who protested the most. He wanted the money put in the disciple's treasury so that he could steal from it. In an instant, Mary's face goes from pure joy and excitement to one of embarrassment and sadness. She had wanted to do something special for the one she loved and those around her mocked her act of worship.

It is Jesus who rose to her defense. "Leave her alone," said Jesus. "Why are you bothering her? She has done a beautiful thing to me." (v.6) He rebukes the disciples and praises what she has done. He understands her heart and is honored by the gift. Living only two miles from Jerusalem in the town of Bethany, Mary may have feared the dangers for Jesus in Jerusalem. She wants to use this opportunity to show her love while there is still time. Jesus acknowledges what lies ahead in the next week when he proclaims "she poured perfume on my body beforehand to prepare for my burial." (v.8) The gift of the perfume is not a waste because it gives honor and love to Jesus. It will be remembered for years to come as a great act of love.

Love given in a timely manner has power. Sometimes the greatest gifts are the ones that we give on the spur of the moment. We see a neighbor struggling to shovel their driveway and we stop to help. We stay overnight with a friend suddenly alone in the hospital. Love isn't always calculated and it often doesn't come at times that fit easily into our schedules. It sees a need and it reaches out because we love Jesus. It helps when help is needed not when it is easiest for us. It often comes with sacrifices of our time and money at the most inconvenient times. Such love has great power because it came at a time when people needed it the most. Such love has power because it came from our heart and not our mind. Love freely given can change lives.

Love given from the heart is remembered. "I tell you the truth, wherever the gospel is preached throughout the world, what she has done will also be told, in memory of her." (v.9) Three of the four gospels tell this story. It must have been a memory that stuck with the disciples for years. This act of worship has encouraged millions of people to show love and kindness to others. We often complain about the coldness or selfishness of the world. What we forget is that we have the power to change a piece of the world with the love of Jesus. One act of selfless love can change the course of a person's life. It can inspire them to love others and it surely will be remembered for years. Change often happens as one person touches another with love and they in turn touch others with the love that they have received from Jesus through people like you and me.

- What the most beautiful thing that you have you seen one person do for another? What were some of the lasting results of this simple act of kindness?

03 What Did You Expect? - Luke 19:28-44

Context: On Palm Sunday, the Sunday before His death, Jesus rode into town fulfilling the Old Testament prophecies about the Messiah. He rode down the hill on the eastern side of Jerusalem in full view of the city. Some cheered him and chanted their support. Others were appalled by this display. We can pray for days and our loved one doesn't get any better. We can pray for a better job or for a better relationship with our spouse. Somehow, it doesn't seem to happen, either. In the end, we get mad at God because He didn't meet our expectations. Our problem is that our expectations are not built around the real Jesus. We try to fit Him into our mold instead of seeing the genuine article and letting Him bring the help that only He can give. The Prince of Peace can change our lives and bring real joy, but we need to let Him give the peace and healing that He has chosen for us. Like the people on Palm Sunday, we often want one kind of peace and Jesus wants to give us something far better and more lasting.

As Jesus comes down the hill toward Jerusalem, many

cheered for a king. "Blessed is the king who comes in the name of the Lord!" "Peace in heaven and glory in the highest!" (v.38) Pilgrims who had come to Jerusalem lined the road shouting and waving palm branches because the "Son of David" (Matt. 21:9) had come to town. They wanted a peace that would liberate them from the oppressive Romans. Their idea of peace would come when this powerful Messiah who cured the sick, fed the crowds and even raised the dead brought political victory to His people. The cheers, however, were temporary. Few understood the real peace that Jesus had come to bring. He had come to conquer sin and not conquer Rome.

The Pharisees thought that the crowd's words were blasphemy. They heard cheers for a Messiah and felt that Jesus was a fraud. The Pharisees jeered Him and commanded Him, "Teacher, rebuke your disciples!" (v.39) Their idea of peace was to get along with the Romans. A counterfeit Messiah coming into town with thousands of followers cheering Him as King might provoke a massacre by the Roman soldiers. Jesus' reply seems to point back to

Habakkuk 2:11 where Habakkuk had prophesied that even the stones of Jerusalem would cry out about the sins of the people. The Jews would face judgment because of sin. Only a Savior from sin could bring real peace.

One would have expected Jesus to be beaming with pride at the cheers of the people on His arrival. Instead, we find tears. "As he approached Jerusalem and saw the city, he wept over it" (v.41) After three years of teaching, the people still did not understand their need for a Savior. He would clear the den of thieves in God's house. He would be rejected by many who did not understand God's plan of salvation. Finally, He saw God's city and wept over the terrible judgment that would come to the city and the temple in just 40 years. Jerusalem and its people would be destroyed because they rejected the one who came to save them and bring God's peace.

Our expectations must be built on the real Jesus. There are still people who cheer for Jesus as the great teacher or healer, but who don't really feel that they need a savior to help them with their sin. There are also many who jeer at Jesus because they reject Him totally. These people feel that they need no

God and no savior since they have technology and science. It is no wonder Jesus still sheds tears. The real Jesus is a friend who wants to heal and teach, but who came most of all to save. Caught in sin, we should cheer that we have a savior who has paid for our sin. We should cheer that He helps us overcome the sins that keep us in bondage. Jesus is our king because He has freed us from our burdens and brings us to the temple in heaven where we can be close to our God.

The crowds were looking for another King David who would bring about a time of peace and prosperity for them. They wanted someone who would heal their illnesses and give them abundant bread. Yet, such a king would not last. Just as the first David died; a political messiah would die and his kingdom would only wither away. God sends a better Messiah who brings an eternal peace. Jesus is available to all generations. He is a king who has dealt with the human condition and not just its symptoms. He is a savior who has taken away the guilt and allows us to be in the presence of our God. He will always be with us to answer our prayers and to help us with the problems that the world brings our way. We should never try to make Jesus fill our mold. We need to take the time to see the real Jesus and let Him give us all the peace and blessings that can come only from Him.

- What reception would Jesus get if He came into your town today? What would the crowds want from Jesus? What would you be looking for?

04 Jesus Predicts His Death-John 12:20-36

Context: On Monday, Jesus takes the disciples into Jerusalem. Having cleansed the temple, Jesus begins to teach the disciples once again about His death and resurrection. The time is so near and the disciples still do not understand what is to come.

Are you comfortable? It is a question that I have been wrestling with lately. I have a great wife and three wonderful children. I have a nice home and a great part of the country to live in. I like my church and the people seem to like me. I do believe that I am comfortable. Yet, is that really what being a Christian is all about? The bible does not promise us a good life or a contented life. It tells us that we must follow our Lord and do whatever brings glory to Him. That often means sacrifice and a little discomfort. But the sacrifice is worth it if our lives bring glory to God so that someone notices the Lord and is saved. In this text, we see that God's glory is why Jesus came to earth. His example teaches us to live our life to His glory and lets God bring a measure of comfort to us.

Jesus knew that there could be no glory without suffering. Glory will only come because He is willing to die for the salvation of all mankind. He illustrates this truth by talking about the "death" of a seed. "I tell you the truth unless a kernel of wheat falls to the ground and dies, it remains only a single seed. But if it dies, it produces many seeds". (v.24) A seed has to be buried in the ground and "die" so that a plant may grow and produce a multitude of seeds. Jesus' death and burial would bring forth fruit in the lives of God's people. He made the sacrifice so that others might live and give glory to God the Father. His death brought God's love to light so we might love God as well.

Just because Jesus knew how wonderful the end result would be, doesn't mean that it was easy. The human Jesus knew how painful it would be. He says, "Now my heart is troubled, and what shall I say? 'Father, save me from this hour'? No, it was for this very reason I came to this hour. Father, glorify your name!" (v.27-28) Even the pain could not deter Him from bringing salvation to us. The cross left Jesus only two choices. He could either ask God to save Him or He could ask the

Father to bring glory from the cross so that the sacrifice would not be wasted. Jesus chose to ask for the Father's glory. The salvation of mankind was the very reason that He had come to the earth. He dreaded the cross, but He wanted our salvation even more.

At that moment, the Father replied from heaven. "Then a voice came from heaven, "I have glorified it, and will glorify it again." (v.28) Jesus had lifted His voice to heaven and the people heard the response from the Father. Through the ministry of Jesus, the Father had brought people closer to Himself. The upcoming sacrifice on the cross would bring glory by drawing others into God's kingdom and salvation. Jesus was doing the Father's work and God wanted everyone to know that truth. The Father and the Son were working in concert so that the name of God might be glorified and so people might come to be saved by the cross. The glory of the Father would come as people believed and were redeemed.

Our lives will never be full unless we are willing to seek God's glory and not our own. Our lives are like seeds, small and insignificant, that can be planted to yield a great harvest by our Lord. Little acts of kindness and service can bring people to faith and change lives. Our lives are to follow our Lord's example. Most of us will not be asked to sacrifice our lives to give God glory. Yet, we will be asked to sacrifice our time to help a child, our talents to provide a service to a neighbor in need, or even our resources so that His ministry is done in our church or community. We give away the things that make life comfortable so that others might learn about our Lord through us and might draw close to Him. We die to self so others can live for God.

Because Jesus was lifted up on the cross, we lift Him up in our lives. Jesus is the center of our lives because of His sacrifice for us. His willingness to suffer for us shows us His love and draws us to Him. We react in love because He loved us first. Those who glorify the Lord will find that other people will be drawn to them as well. People will appreciate us for the sacrifices that we make. We will feel a great satisfaction as we change the lives of those around us for the Lord. When we see the needs of others and use our gifts, it gives us a purpose in life. We see their need and offer to help. Our love gives glory to the Lord and leads people to Him.

- What sacrifice in your life would make the most difference for those that you love? What holds you back from giving glory to the Lord by serving others?

05 Satan Plots, But Jesus Is in Control - Luke 22:1-13

Context: In a town flooded with religious pilgrims and Jewish spies, Jesus would like to share some private time with His disciples. Satan wants to disrupt this private time of teaching and fellowship, but Jesus shows that He is in control of the events of this week.

The news media is filled with reports of violence and evil in our world. We hear of attacks of guerrillas in foreign lands and tornados wiping out whole towns in the Midwest. Closer to home, we see on Facebook that a family in the neighborhood getting a divorce or a dear friend is having a sudden and unexpected heart attack. We begin to wonder if anyone or anything is safe. Evil seems to swirl around us and destroy lives. Our emotions shout for God to do more to protect His people against this threat. Our faith reminds us that God is near. Evil may look like it is in control, but it is really our God who controls the world. He wants the maximum benefit for His people.

The Jewish leaders felt mocked by Jesus all week. On Sunday, He had ridden into town on a colt while the crowds waved palm branches and called Him "king" (Luke 18:38). On Monday, Jesus had the audacity to come and clear out their temple proclaiming them to be robbers. They had questioned His authority and been ridiculed before the crowds by this upstart rabbi. The Jewish leaders had enough of this man. "The chief priests and the teachers of the law were looking for some way to get rid of Jesus, for they were afraid of the people." (v.2) Jesus had to go, but how? Jerusalem was packed with people who admired Him. A riot would bring bloodshed from the Romans.

Judas solved their problem for them. He had followed Jesus for years thinking that he could ride the coattails of this rabbi to the top of the Jewish hierarchy. Yet, recently he had been rebuked by Jesus when Mary had wasted precious perfume in the worship of Jesus. Then Jesus had failed to take advantage of the fervor of the crowds that ushered Him into Jerusalem. Judas was fed up. "And Judas went to the chief priests and the officers of the temple guard and discussed with them how he might betray Jesus." (v.4) What a "godsend" it was to have

an inside man come to them ready to betray his master. Here

was one who could tell them how and when to capture Jesus

away from the crowds. All they had to do was wait for the right

time.

The perfect place to capture Jesus would have been at the

last supper. It was an upper room that could be surrounded

and it would be easy to overpower the few disciples. Jesus

seemed to know the plans of his enemies. He gives directions

to the place for the supper in such a way that even Judas

cannot know where they will meet. "He replied, "As you enter

the city, a man carrying a jar of water will meet you. Follow

him to the house that he enters," (v.10) Men rarely carried

pitchers of water. That was work for the women. This unknown

man would lead Peter and John to the room where Jesus

could hold the Last Supper. Only Peter and John would know

where the room was before they all met. Jesus was fully in

control of the time of His betrayal.

Jesus did not let evil take away His time of teaching and

fellowship with His disciples. Evil men could plan, but Jesus was in control. He wanted to show His love and give the disciples encouragement and instructions before He died on the cross. Evil will come because we live in a sinful world filled with sinful people. Our own sin will cause others and ourselves pain as well. Yet, Jesus often shapes the time when those things come so that we have the least damage and the most gain. He can use pain to teach us and strengthen our faith. He can use a tragedy to bring families and friends together at the time when they need each other most. Even when there is evil, Jesus is still in control of the people He loves.

What would the story have looked like if Judas had been allowed to betray Jesus at the Last Supper? The sacrament of Holy Communion might not have been given. Jesus would not have had the opportunity to give the teachings of John 13-16. Jesus would not have been able to prepare for crucifixion with hours of prayer in the Garden of Gethsemane. Yet, it did not happen that way because God works visibly and invisibly to control the plans of evil in our lives. The betrayal came at the moment that Jesus had planned so that His preparation for the disciples and for us would be complete. Evil events and people will come in every person's life. We need to trust Jesus with our future. We know that He can control evil to get the maximum benefit for His people.

- Where does your world seem out of control right now? What parts of your life do you need to give to Jesus in prayer so that He can control them and help you?

06 The Joy of Serving-John 13 1-17

Context: Knowing that the cross was near, Jesus got up and began the lowly task of washing His disciple's feet even as the food was being served. It was the task of the lowest servant, but none of the disciples had taken up the task. Here, Jesus will show what it means to be a child of God.

Tom laid on his deathbed with his family gathered around him. There were so many things that he wanted to tell them because he knew this might be his last day. He wanted to encourage his son Luke to hold on through a difficult time in his career. He wanted Mary to not be afraid to put her career aside and take care of her young children. Most of all, he wanted to tell his wife Jill how much she meant to him. Knowing that the cross is near, Jesus gives a farewell message to His disciples in John 13-17. The disciples have been arguing about who is the greatest (Luke 22:24) and so Jesus begins His message with an object lesson in humility and service. Service is about lifting others up because we love them as Jesus has loved us.

The disciples must have been shocked when they saw Jesus get up from the supper, put aside his outer garments and take up a towel and a basin of water to wash their feet. This was the task of the lowest slave. No dinner guest, let alone the master, would stoop to such a task. Yet, a person who loves another and wants to show that love will wash feet and do even more. "Having loved his own who were in the world, he now showed them the full extent of his love." (v.1) Service often comes because of love. Jesus has grown close to these men. He knows what they will face in the hours ahead as they watch Him arrested and as many of them will cower in fear when He is crucified. His action shows how important they are to Him and sets up powerfully the words He will speak to them that night.

Yet, service is not always taken well. The disciples are often pictured at a U-shaped table with Jesus and John at one end and Peter at the other. Peter had watched Jesus wash the feet of all eleven of the other disciples but struggles when it is his turn. "He came to Simon Peter, who said to him, Lord, are you going to wash my feet?" (v.6) Brazen Peter will try to tell the

Lord what to do. First, he tells the Lord not to wash him. Then he commands the Lord to wash all of him so that he is closer to Jesus than all the other disciples. What started as an act of love has now become a scene of conflict and probably resentment as the other disciples hear what Peter is saying. Jesus calmly explains what His service is about and Peter's feet are washed like the other eleven.

It is at those times that we need to remember that service comes from strength, not weakness. "Jesus knew that the Father had put all things under his power and that he had come from God."(v.3) Jesus' service came from His strength, not from any compulsion. He did not need to earn the favor of the disciples. He served them because of His character and His love. He served them because He had a gift that He wanted to give them. He had a lesson that He wanted to pass on so that their lives would be better. If Jesus had never washed their feet that night, no one would have noticed and no one would have cared. He got up and served them because He could and because He wanted to change their lives.

So what is the lesson that Jesus has for us? One lesson is that service elevates us and dignifies others. He set the pattern of service here and is honored for it. "Now that I, your Lord and Teacher, have washed your feet, you also should wash one another's feet." (v.14) He was honored as their Lord and Teacher because of all the service that He had given to them over the years. If they wanted to be honored by others, they would give such service as well. In the book of Acts, we see the disciples lifting people out of the gutter as they heal and teach. People then and today honor such servants because of what they did in the name of Jesus. Service doesn't humiliate us. Humble service makes us important to others because of what we have done for them. As we help and lift others up, we are lifted up in the eyes of others as well. As a camper, I have seen two kinds of camping families. There are families where everyone pitches in to set up camp and cook the meals. Each person knows their job and as they work together, the task goes easier and the family enjoys their time together. Then there are families where dad and mom do all the work and the kids play video games. Dad yells at the kids and the kids complain about "being out in nature". No one is happy there. Real happiness comes when we serve others because of Jesus. It can be Mom, Dad, and the kids or it can be a church family that works together and everyone uses their gifts. Happiness comes with service because we work together and gain the respect of others. Service lifts us up even as we lift others up with our service.

- Who has done something for you that you are eternally grateful for? Who could you serve today so that you could make a similar difference in their lives?

07 Kindness Among Cruelty-Matthew 26:20-30

Context: As the twelve disciples were seated around the last supper table, Jesus reveals that one of them will betray Him. Jesus exposes Judas during a meal of close fellowship. Jesus has loved them and it will be one of His own that Satan will turn against Jesus.

"I can't believe he said that! He stabbed me in the back right in front of the boss. I'll get even with him for that." Suddenly you spend the whole day upset as you replay the event in your mind. You become rude to others who you think should have stood up for you. You feel like all the world is against you. You start worrying about your job and you begin to plan how to get back in the boss's good graces and get even with the "friend" who did you wrong. One rude comment or action by another person can ruin your whole week. It doesn't have to be that way. You can counteract rudeness with kindness. You can follow the example of Jesus. He was kind when He was betrayed by a friend.

It was an act of friendship to eat bread together in Jewish

circles. Here were the twelve disciples sitting together with Jesus at the Passover meal. Judas was sitting on the Lord's left in a place of honor at the feast sharing the morsels of bread with his master. Without any warning, Jesus would announce that one of them was a betrayer. "Jesus replied, "The one who has dipped his hand into the bowl with me will betray me." (v.23) The disciples were in shock. Each of them asked if they were the one who would unknowingly betray Jesus. Even Judas asked if he was the betrayer. Jesus simply answered, "Yes, it is you." (v.25) Jesus had shown nothing but kindness and was now being stabbed in the back by one of his "friends".

Jesus could have yelled and screamed about not being appreciated, but instead, He gave His friends a great gift. He gave them the sacrament. In giving them His body and blood in and with the bread and wine, He was giving them and all the church a gift straight from the cross. He said to them as He gave them the third cup, "This is my blood of the covenant, which is poured out for many for the forgiveness of sins." (v.28) The third of four cups at the Passover symbolized the third promise of Exodus 6:6-7. This was the promise of redemption. In this meal, Christians still receive the forgiveness that Jesus won for them on the cross. The disciples could share this meal "in remembrance" (1 Cor. 11:25) of what Jesus had done for them in love. They could be forgiven because of His sacrifice.

Jesus finished the meal by reminding them that His death was not the end. "I tell you, I will not drink of this fruit of the vine from now on until that day when I drink it anew with you in my Father's kingdom."(v.29) He would rise from the dead and be with them for forty days after His resurrection. He would show Himself to them and teach them so that they would understand the meaning of this sacrifice and victory. Jesus would even bring them to be with Him in heaven. They were His friends and He would not desert them or retaliate against them for their weaknesses and their sins. Jesus would be faithful to them, even though most of them would abandon Him as He died on the cross. They could count on Him. He was sacrificing Himself for their future.

You just can't let one person hurt you so much that you lash out at everyone else. We are to remain kind in a cruel world.

Show kindness when you are hurt and disarm the situation.

Your boss may be impressed with your kindness and

character. Your coworkers or friends may be surprised when

you do not make the situation worse by a fit of anger. Let

God's character guide you so you are kind and generous to

others the rest of the day. It is hard, I know. Yet, responding

with kindness helps everyone else to forget your mistakes and

remember the many kindnesses that you shared each day.

You don't have to get even. Let your character and your

thoughtfulness make you valued to others.

Christ wants us to show His love to the world around us.

People around us are having "bad days" all the time. A

Christian can spread a lot of love by just bringing the kindness

of Jesus to their world. Smile at the clerk at Wal-Mart and ask

how their day has gone. You will be surprised how you change

their whole day just because you cared. Tip your server at the

restaurant well and be sure to be courteous and smile at them.

They often have rough days too when customers treat them

badly. Smile when you come home and ask your spouse how

his or her day was. Show you are interested in what they do. Kindness can change the people around you. It can help them on a day when they want to lash out in anger.

- Take up the challenge and smile at your co-workers, your family and even the server at lunch. When they ask you how your day has been, just tell them that God has been good to you.

08 When Satan Sifts You-Luke 22:14-38

Context: Judas was not the only one who would fail Jesus as He prepared to die. Satan was ready to destroy the other disciples even as Jesus prepared for the cross. In an act of love, Jesus predicts Peter's betrayal and return to leadership so that the darkness ahead does not destroy his faith.

There are times that you just want to kick yourself. You get angry at a fellow Christian when they let you down. You get jealous when you see the success of another's ministry. You get caught in a terrible sin when others thought you were a servant of God. We think that Christians should be above that for we have experienced the love of Jesus. We should have put all that behind us. Oddly, the disciples hadn't become perfect either. Jesus tells one of them, "Simon, Simon, Satan has asked to sift you as wheat" (v.31) Jesus was warning Peter and the other disciples that the enemy was on the prowl. Peter was a brave man, but Satan would attack him and his courage would fail. Satan will sift us as well when we do God's work. We have to be ready for his assault.

Judas was already losing the battle with Satan. Jesus would show love and kindness in the sacrament at this meal. Judas had already felt evil's power as he prepared to hand over the flesh of Jesus to Satan. Jesus warns Judas not to give in. "The Son of Man will go as it has been decreed, but woe to that man who betrays him." (v.22) There was still time to repent and not fall to Satan. God the Father would figure out another path taking Jesus to the cross. Judas had walked with Jesus for years and felt the heart of his Savior. Yet, he got up from the table that night and went to the chief priests to arrange the betrayal in the garden. Satan had sifted Judas and captured his soul. He would be lost to the kingdom and would be replaced (Acts 1:15-22).

The other disciples were also losing the purpose of discipleship and service. "Also, a dispute arose among them as to which of them was considered to be greatest." (v.24) It was not the first time that they had argued about who was the greatest. Jesus had to explain that they were thinking like the unsaved gentiles instead of being servants of God. They had given into the Jewish thinking that the Messiah was going to restore the glory of King David (Matt. 21:9). As Jesus the

Messiah had chosen them to be His disciples, they argued

who would get the most important positions in the

government. Did they not understand the example He had

given in washing their feet? (John 13:1-17) Satan had sifted

the eleven disciples and was making them think of self and not

serving others.

Peter gets a special warning following the dispute over who

was the greatest. "Jesus answered, "I tell you, Peter, before

the rooster crows today, you will deny three times that you

know me." (v.34) Peter's boast is a warning that none of us

knows their own heart or the power of Satan. Peter was

courageous and was the leader of the disciples. Satan would

target him so that the other disciples would be discouraged.

Within a few hours, the leader of the disciples would fail his

master Jesus. Yet, unlike Judas, Peter would not lose his

faith. Jesus specifically asks Peter to strengthen the others in

their hour of need. Satan would sift Peter and bring him to his

knees, but Peter would be restored and would lead many

others to faith in Jesus.

Jesus had eagerly desired this night with them (v.15). They were precious to Him and He would help them with the temptations that they faced. He tells them that He has prayed for them (v.32). He will also pray for them again this night (John 17:6-19). His cross will bring forgiveness and the eleven will be restored to service. Our temptation is to think that we can no longer serve if we fail our Lord. As we see around the Last Supper table, that is not true. Satan will sift all the servants of the Lord and may even pick the strongest "Peters" among us for greater sifting. Our hope is in Jesus. He prays for us. He warns us. He even can give us the strength to overcome the severest sifting.

Was there ever any hope for them that night? Yes, I think there was one. I think that they could have drawn strength through prayer. Jesus had been praying for them and asked them to pray for themselves so that they would not fall into temptation (Luke 22:40). Satan will try to sift us, but God is stronger. Just as Jesus received strength in His prayer (Luke 22:43), the Father would have strengthened the disciples. When we bathe our lives and ministries in prayer, it makes it harder for Satan to overcome us. Our eyes and thoughts are focused on the Lord and not on ourselves. Yet, even then we may fall. In those moments, we can take comfort that the Lord will forgive and restore us just as He did Peter and the others.

- Where have you felt Satan sifting you so that you are discouraged or selfish? What difference would praying about your life and ministry daily with the Lord make for you? What aspect of your life do you need to talk about with Him now?

09 The Way To God-John 14:1-14

Context: The Passover meal was over and Jesus begins to prepare the disciples for the evening ahead. The arrest in the garden, the trials, and the cross would rock their faith. He begins the discussion with a promise. I am leaving to prepare a place for you.

The Last Supper meal was not a picnic or fun family gathering. It was a very stressful evening for the disciples. During the meal, Jesus announced to them that He was leaving them. Panic must have ensued. What should have been a time of celebration became a time of terror and questions. You know the feeling. Such fears have become an epidemic in our society. The bookstores are filled with books dealing with topics like "When you feel like a failure" or "Stop trying to do it all". Our weakness and failures knock us down on a regular basis. We often try to ignore them. We may even deny that we have problems. Jesus brings comfort in this text. He wants us to turn to Him instead of denying our weakness. He promises to help.

He wants you to know that He has the future covered. "In my Father's house are many rooms; if it were not so, I would have told you. I am going there to prepare a place for you." (v.2) The disciples are afraid. Just when it seemed like everything was going well, life fell apart. The triumph of Palm Sunday had degenerated into Jesus' discussion that He would be a casualty of the cause. If He was to die, was there any hope for them? The answer is a resounding yes. Jesus is going so that the disciples will have a future. He is going so that He can prepare a place for them. He will prepare a place so that they can be with Jesus and with the Father forever. They will never have to worry about being separated from Him or His love again.

They would be safe in this life, too, because God would walk with them. As Jews, they believed that it was God who protected them from the evil of the world. The Almighty God protected His people when they left Egypt. Jesus wanted them to see that God had been walking with them as He had the Jews and would continue to do so. Anyone who has seen me has seen the Father. How can you say, 'Show us the Father'?

(v.9) For the last three years, they had lived with God. God was the friend and teacher whom they had committed their lives to. As they walked with Jesus, they had walked with God. God had personally taught them and cared for them. They were closer to God than virtually anyone else since the time of Moses.

Just because Jesus was leaving did not mean that Jesus wouldn't listen whenever they asked for help. While Jesus had been with them, they had been free to ask Him questions and talk about their fears. His death wouldn't change that. He promises them "I will do whatever you ask in my name so that the Son may bring glory to the Father." (v.13) His death would not be final. After He ascended into heaven, they could still talk to Him through the gift of prayer. Jesus would be beside them in ministry and in life. He would be able to listen and help them through every need. He would comfort them. They just needed to trust Him when He was in heaven as they had trusted Him on earth. In prayer, He would listen and would conquer their worries and their fears.

We are often overwhelmed by doubt and inner conflict when

troubles come upon us. Strength evaporates and we find ourselves weighed down. At such times, we have two choices. We can give in to fear or we can turn to Jesus trusting Him to help. The scriptures give us many reasons to trust Jesus and to look to Him for help. "I am the way and the truth and the life. No one comes to the Father except through me." (v.6) is our promise that all the power of God is available through Jesus. I picture Jesus telling me, "Calm down, haven't I helped you in the past?" I know that there is nothing that Jesus cannot deal with. I have to come to Him trusting that He will help me. My choice is to feel terror apart from Him or find peace when I look to Him.

Those who have the comfort of Jesus can be a comfort to others. Jesus makes a promise, I tell you the truth, anyone who has faith in me will do what I have been doing. He will do even greater things than these." (v.12). The promise is that the disciples will affect more people in their lives than Jesus had in His three years of ministry. At first, that seems impossible, yet Peter preached on Pentecost and 3000 were saved in one day. Paul would convert people in Turkey, Greece, and Rome.

Those who have the comfort of Jesus can spread that comfort to their communities. Picture a world filled with Christians trusting in Jesus and bringing that comfort into the lives of their family, friends, and coworkers. Pain and suffering would find healing and help for so many. The comfort of Jesus is powerful. It can change our lives and the lives of those around us.

- Where do you feel like a failure in life right now? When was the last time you brought that problem to the Lord in prayer?

10 Why Are We Here? - John 15:1-17

Context: This is the seventh and last "I am" statement in the gospel of John. With a picture from the vineyard, Jesus teaches them about the blessings they have enjoyed by being close to Him and the responsibility that they have to remain in Him tonight and forever.

Why are you here? What were the expectations of your parents when they fed you and nurtured you? Did they want you to be a baseball player, a concert pianist or an engineer? I am sure that your parents gave direction and perhaps spent money on a baseball glove or an upright piano. They had dreams and wanted something special for you because they loved you. God has dreams for you as well. He feeds and nurtures every one of His children with an end in mind. As Jesus is giving his farewell speech to the disciples, he shares some insight into God's dreams for every Christian. He tells how God nurtures us and what God expects of all of us. He tells of His hope for us.

In order that we might bear fruit, God nourishes us. Grapes

need to be cared for with water and fertilizer. People need physical and spiritual nourishment as well. "If you remain in me and my words remain in you, ask whatever you wish, and it will be given you." (v.7) Jesus promises to give us what we need. He is the one we can call on when we are struggling financially or when our health fails us. You don't have to beg Him to care for you. He will provide the food that our bodies and our souls need. Jesus will even give special care when circumstances demand it. He wants us to be strong and healthy so that we thrive even when the world around us is not conducive to growth.

His pruning and nourishment are also given so that we bear fruit. "This is to my Father's glory, that you bear much fruit, showing yourselves to be my disciples" (v.8) Fruit is not an option for the Christian. God does not expect us to sit around and produce nothing for the kingdom. It is true that there will be times when we will produce abundant fruit because times are ideal. Other times fruit will be less because times are hard. In all times, there will be fruit. It may be the fruit of character so that others see that God's children are kind or honest. It may be the fruit of actions in which God's people will help others and nourish them as God has nourished us. It will, however, always be fruit for others and not for us. A grape plant produces fruit for others to eat. Our fruit is to benefit others just as God has cared for us.

Such fruit is possible only if you remain in Jesus. We are not expected to produce fruit by our own strength or resources. "Remain in me, and I will remain in you. No branch can bear fruit by itself; it must remain in the vine. Neither can you bear fruit unless you remain in me." (v.4) Those who remain in fellowship with Jesus will be healthy and produce fruit. They draw strength from Jesus because they have cultivated a deep relationship with Him. They are the people who daily take time for the word. Prayer is intimate and is a place where they touch the heart of God. They remain in the Lord because they know that they cannot thrive in this world without Him. A day doesn't go right without Bible study and prayer. They have to be attached to Jesus in order to thrive from His strength. Why are we here? The answer is to produce fruit. Yet that is not always easy. It means that we have to take time from our busy lives to be in the word. It means that God has to prune our lives so we can bear fruit and that can be painful. He may remove distractions and activities in our life or painfully cut off things that are sinful and destroying to us or others. There are times that I am sure most of us just want God to go away and leave us alone. Yet, that would be the greatest judgment that God could give. To abandon us and let us have our own way is to let our lives be filled with things that will hurt us. If God were to abandon us, we would wander in life instead of having a clear path. Pruning is necessary for us to produce fruit and for us to have joy.

God wants His children to be different. He wants them to be filled with power and with love. "My command is this: Love each other as I have loved you." (v.12) The disciples would surprise the Sanhedrin with their knowledge and their power (Acts 4:13). They would show love to beggars (Acts 3:6) and for each other (Acts 12:12). God pours Himself into us so that we can bring His love into the world by our actions and character. As we remain in Him, we bear fruit giving life a purpose. We show the love and power of our Lord to our world that needs Him more than ever. God has great dreams for His people. Remain in Him and life will be satisfying.

- What dreams does God have for you? What needs to be pruned from you in order for those dreams to happen?

11 Swimming Against the Current-John 15:18-27

Context: One would expect that the Messiah would be loved by all the Jewish people. Sadly, many did not want the true Messiah and would try to destroy His disciples as well. The hours ahead would demonstrate the hatred of the world for the Messiah and show what lied ahead for the disciples as well. I have always been intrigued with salmon fighting their way up the streams to spawn. The water resists them. The dams block their way. The bears scoop them up for food. It would be easier to just stay in the ocean, but they will not. They have a mission and they will not give it up. Christians have to swim upstream against our culture's beliefs on attitudes and lifestyles. We are told that anything from the Bible is old-fashioned or narrow-minded. What is even more alarming is that you will be considered weird if you return love for hatred or if you do something kind or generous. A few may think you are a hero for caring, but a lot of friends will think your sacrifice is stupid. Being a Christian means being out of sync with the world a lot of the time.

Around the Last Supper table, Jesus reminded the disciples about the world's hatred. For three years, He traveled and showed amazing kindness. He healed people whose lives were torn apart by sickness. He talked with people who were confused and frustrated and showed them the God's truth. There were tens of thousands of people whose lives were touched and changed by Jesus, yet the world hated Him. "If I had not done among them what no one else did, they would not be guilty of sin. But now they have seen these miracles, and yet they have hated both me and my Father." (v.24) Ultimately, the religious leaders would have Him put to death. The reason was twofold. They hated Him because He told the truth. They hated Him even more because His great love showed how wicked they really were.

The disciples had chosen to belong to Jesus. They enjoyed His love and kindness. They enjoyed the things that He had taught them. The community that Jesus was creating called the church was a place of fellowship and belonging. Being so close to Jesus had an effect. "If you belonged to the world, it would love you as its own. As it is, you do not belong to the world, but I have chosen you out of the world." (v.19) Jesus

had taken them out of the world and contact with Him was

changing them. They no longer thought like the world and

were not trapped in Satan's lies. They were a people who had

learned to care for one another and who lifted others up. Their

ideas and actions were different and showed that they

belonged to Jesus.

Because they belonged to Jesus and acted like Jesus, they

would be hated by the world. "They will treat you this way

because of my name, for they do not know the One who sent

me." (v.21) Jesus was warning the disciples and all believers

what lies ahead. The disciples would be taken before the

Sanhedrin for speaking about Jesus and for healing people.

Their words and actions demonstrated God's power and love

frightening the pious religious leaders who wanted it stopped.

The early church would face the same hazards. Paul will be

stripped, beaten and thrown in prison for casting the demon

out of a slave girl. His kindness was rewarded with

accusations and physical abuse. Early Christians would die by

the tens of thousands for worshipping God instead of

emperors and Roman gods. They were all out of sync with the world in which they lived and they would be hated for it.

We feel the pain of the apostles and sometimes we want to just give up swimming against the tide. We will be tempted to compromise. We will be tempted to say something even if we don't mean it to get along with others. It would be easy to do so, but the Spirit helps us to see that such behavior is not wise. "When the Counselor comes, whom I will send to you from the Father, the Spirit of truth who goes out from the Father, he will testify about me." (v.26) The Holy Spirit reminds us that the tide is all heading for destruction. Alternative lifestyles, greed, anger, and a host of other culturally acceptable sins cause a lot of pain and destruction. It may be hard, but following Jesus is the only way of happiness and life. Much of where the culture leads results in ruin. Only Jesus has the way of life.

If swimming upstream for yourself is not motivation enough, then swim upstream for those you love. Lust, anger, and lies so common in our culture destroy families and individuals around you. You need to be different so that you don't destroy the ones you love with sin. You need to be different so that you can encourage them to swim upstream as well. We encourage each other every Sunday morning and pray together for God's help along the path. Swimming upstream together creates a swell that makes it easier to go against the current of our culture. What we do impacts our children, our friends, and our neighbors. Like the salmon swimming upstream, we do it together and we have a purpose that keeps us going in spite of the struggle.

- Where do you find it hard to swim against the current of our culture? Who do you know who could swim by your side encouraging you and keeping you accountable so that you continue along God's path?

12 Let The Spirit Work-John 16:5-15

Context: Having told the disciples of the coming persecution, Jesus wants them to know that He is sending someone powerful to help them. The task of spreading the gospel would not be easy, but the Spirit would overcome the world.

Jesus must have been fun to watch. His disciples had ringside seats for His ministry of healing the sick, battling demons and teaching thousands. Yet, He had announced at the Last Supper that He was going to leave them. "Now I am going to him who sent me, yet none of you asks me, 'Where are you going?' (v.5) Panic filled their hearts. He was giving them the ministry. How could they cast out demons or preach the message? They didn't feel ready. For most of us, it is still scary. We feel no more ready than they were. We go out and hire a pastor to do ministry. Yet, the Bible says that it is our job and our responsibility. Fortunately, there is help from Jesus and that help comes from the Holy Spirit.

It will not always be easy. The first challenge is that the world doesn't want to believe. The disciples faced a Roman world with its own group of "superhero" gods and Jews that had

remade the true God into someone who would serve them as

they pleased. The Holy Spirit would help the disciples to attack

this unbelief "in regard to sin, because men do not believe in

me;" (v.9) Both groups needed to see the truth. The Roman

gods were not helping them. Romans had fashioned gods

after their own nature. These "superman gods" didn't seem to

care about people or provide help for the present or future.

The Jewish leaders had remade God into someone who cared

for the elite and not the common man. People were amazed to

hear about the true God who loved them and would really

help.

The disciples would show them a new future by showing them

the ascended Savior. The Holy Spirit would help people

believe in a God that they could no longer see or walk with. He

would convict them "in regard to righteousness, because I am

going to the Father, where you can see me no longer;" (v.10)

If you look in the book of Acts, these disciples would

constantly talk about Jesus. For the person whose life is not

working, they would present the solution. Jesus could help

people through the toughest difficulties of life. Jesus had the future on earth and in heaven firmly in His hands. The disciples would help people by talking about Jesus and letting them share in His hope.

Finally, the lives and actions of the disciples showed the futility of the false gods. Satan was doomed. The Holy Spirit would show God's victory "in regard to judgment, because the prince of this world now stands condemned." (v.11) While Rome thought that their gods could not be stopped from conquering the world, their kingdom was already unraveling. Satan could not deliver on the promises of ease or a happy life that he has made to people. The fall of Rome and the rise of the church would show the truth about the Roman gods and the one true God. The church would prosper because it was built on the love and care of Jesus not the crumbling lies of Satan. As people saw their gods crumble, they realized that Jesus was the only way.

You may be wondering "How do I do all that?" The answer is that Jesus has given us a helper, a guide, and a trailblazer. "But when he, the Spirit of truth, comes, he will guide you into all truth. He will not speak on his own; he will speak only what

he hears, and he will tell you what is yet to come." (v.13). We

have the Holy Spirit to provide us the opportunities and the

words to say when those opportunities present themselves.

The Holy Spirit would put truth together for the disciples on

Pentecost and continue to teach them throughout their lives.

Those who are in the word will find that the Lord continues to

teach us all of our lives. We will know what to say and we will

know when and how to say it. We can lean on Him to help us.

As we look at the disciples, we see the tactic that the Spirit

taught them. They didn't argue doctrine or try to guilt people

into coming to faith with the fear of hell. They told the story of

Jesus and often told stories about what the Lord was doing in

their lives. People today still want to hear what is working.

They will buy a kitchen appliance, or a car based on the

witness of their friends. Our goal should be to tell the stories of

the Bible and the stories of God working in our lives so that

others can see how God changes things and makes things

better. God never calls us to convince them. We just need to

witness. The Holy Spirit will use our stories to work on their hearts. We can change lives just by telling the stories of a Jesus who is worth knowing and believing in.

- What is your favorite story about Jesus from the bible? What is a story from your life you could share? Who needs to hear about your Jesus this coming week?

13 Be Transformed with Joy-John 16:16-33

Context: When the Spirit came, He would turn their sorrow into joy. They would grieve and feel the pain that comes with being a servant of Christ, but the Holy Spirit would help them triumph. They would have joy as they see Jesus again and have a joy that lasts.

The search for pleasure keeps people from real joy. We live in a nation constantly looking for happiness and pleasure. People work long hours just to afford the perfect vacation or a beautiful car. They plan for months to have the perfect wedding or the perfect Christmas. Trouble is that none of those things last very long. The vacation is over in a few days. The car gets boring before we pay it off. Soon we are looking for the next thing that will give us joy. How much would you give for a joy that lasts? Jesus promises us such transformational joy. He promises a joy that He will put inside our hearts. His joy is with you no matter what the circumstances. This joy will last a lifetime and it can all be yours.

What does this joy look like? Jesus uses the example of a woman in childbirth. "A woman giving birth to a child has pain because her time has come, but when her baby is born she forgets the anguish because of her joy that a child is born into the world." (v.21) Having watched my wife in childbirth, I can tell you that it looks very painful. Yet, as soon as that child was put in her arms, the sorrow all turned to a lifetime of joy. The disciples will grieve for Jesus. They will see Him betrayed, tried, and one will see Him dying on a cross. Yet, Easter will come and joy will overtake their grief. The sorrow of the cross will be seen as the path to the joy of forgiveness and salvation. Christians have a joy that lasts a lifetime.

The disciples worried that Jesus' departure meant that their friendship will be gone forever. They have been spoiled to know the joy of having a friend who nurtured them and cared for them. Jesus promises that God the Father will listen to them when they pray. "Until now you have not asked for anything in my name. Ask and you will receive, and your joy will be complete." (v.24) The disciples have a God who loves them and will listen and care for them. They would have the opportunity to talk to God knowing that He would never give them anything that would harm them. Ask in "Jesus' name" means simply to ask for the things that Jesus wants for you. We ask God to make the choice of what we are to get. We do this because we have a God who will only give us things that will be good for us.

Jesus knew that the disciples would face struggles in the months and years ahead. He wanted them to know that He had conquered everything and that He would walk beside them as their friend and helper. He tells them, "I have told you these things, so that in me you may have peace. In this world you will have trouble. But take heart! I have overcome the world." (v.33)As they lived in Him, they would overcome the world as well. They would stand up to demons and to evil leaders. They would overcome the odds and start a movement that is still going strong in the world. Hardship was coming as they served Jesus, but joy would come as well because they would be victorious by the power and presence of Jesus. Worldly joy comes in spurts. We have joy for a moment during a vacation, the purchase of a new toy or a moment of triumph in life. Joy comes through Jesus for a lifetime. This lifetime of joy comes because we have a God who loves us and who promises to be with us always. "The Father himself loves you because you have loved me and have believed that I came from God." (v.27) As people loved by God, we can make a choice to live in His love and joy or to keep running after things that will give us only moments of joy. It takes some time to develop a relationship with the Lord, but that relationship will bring blessings that you can carry with you for a lifetime. God's joy is something that is put on the inside of His people. I think of David chased by Saul, Daniel in the lion's den, or Paul in prison. No one would call what they were going through a reason for joy. Yet they had joy because God was with them. The joys of the world are fleeting because they are things we cannot control or truly own. The joy of the Lord is like a well that springs up inside us. It starts in the heart where the Holy Spirit lives and changes your attitudes and your view of life. You start seeing that God gives you a reason to rejoice. He will care for you all the days of your life and that means that your future is safe. He even wants you to be closer to Him and have that joy every day.

- How has your relationship with the Lord brought you joy? How might you build your relationship with God so that joy might increase?

14 Joy and Victory-John 17:6-18

Context: It is time to leave for the Garden of Gethsemane, but Jesus pauses to pray for the disciples before they go. He knew that they would not pray for themselves in the garden. Here, He prays for their protection and for their mission to the world.

It was a beautiful day in late spring and the seminary graduates were all seated in crisp rows wearing their caps and gowns. Dr. Wilson muttered a prayer of thanks to the Lord as he looked out fondly at the men seated before him. This was a strong class of pastors. He had sat with them at lunch and been amazed at their questions and understanding of scripture. He had felt their passion for ministry and their great love for the Lord. Yet, Dr. Wilson knew the challenges that these men would face as they were sent out across the United States and into foreign mission fields. The world was turning hostile to the faith. "O Lord, protect them and help them as they serve", he prayed. Such must have been the joy and concern of our Lord as He prepared to send His disciples into the world the night before He died.

The cross was near. Jesus looked across the table at the disciples who had spent the last couple years with Him and He rejoiced in their understanding and faith. "For I gave them the words you gave me and they accepted them. They knew with certainty that I came from you, and they believed that you sent me." (v.8) This was not a small feat. Many people had heard the words Jesus had spoken and did not believe. The crowds often found them hard to understand. The Jewish religious leaders rejected His message as heresy. Before Him was a core of people who believed. They would form the basis for the church after His death and resurrection. He rejoiced in their confidence.

Because of that faith, they belonged to the Father and were no longer part of the world. They had trusted in Jesus and had identified themselves as His disciples. Jesus prayed for them with joy, but also with a great deal of apprehension. "I pray for them. I am not praying for the world, but for those you have given me, for they are yours." (v.9) They had become God's children not just in name, but in truth. The crowds followed

Jesus looked for miracles and a bread king. These had given

their lives to Him for three years. The eleven would give the

rest of their lives to the gospel and the salvation of the world.

Their hearts belonged to Him. He loved them and asked the

Father to watch over them in the next trying hours and for the

rest of their lives. He wanted none of them to be lost.

In love, He had given them a special gift. He had given them

the word. "I have given them your word and the world has

hated them, for they are not of the world any more than I am

of the world." (v.14) Three of the men at this table would write

books of what would become part of the New Testament. All

of them would have the message as their own to share with

the world. It would change their lives and separate them from

the world in which they lived. The word would bring the joy of

salvation to many who heard them speak. It would bring power

as these men would do miracles in Jesus' name. Finally, the

word would change the lives of many who heard and accepted

the message just as they had. There was much to celebrate

for Jesus. The Father had done much in the lives of these

men.

Yet, Jesus knew the challenges that these men and every
Christian face. He had protected the disciples in their years
together. Now He was leaving. He asked that the Father
would protect them. "My prayer is not that you take them out
of the world but that you protect them from the evil one." (v.15)
All the blessings from Jesus are tempered by the hostility of
Satan. He doesn't want us invading his kingdom and stealing
his subjects with the power of the gospel. He will use
persecution in all of its forms to stop God's people from
fulfilling their ministry. This prayer of Jesus is indirectly a
prayer for all those who bring the message of salvation to
others. It is Jesus' prayer for the Father's help and protection
as Jesus sends us into the world.

It was for them and for us that Jesus died. The ministry that all
Christ's disciples do needs power if it is to defeat Satan. It has
to have the power of the cross and the resurrection. "For them
I sanctify myself, that they too may be truly sanctified." (v.19)
Jesus closes this part of the prayer with a pledge to give the
disciples that power. He would sanctify the disciples and the

world by the cross. The cross is at the heart of the message that the disciples accepted and proclaimed. The cross would make them His so that Satan and evil could never claim them. Satan might attack, but he can never stand up against the cross. Let us go into the world and change it by the power of the victorious cross of Christ.

- As you look at the members of your church or small group, what would Jesus be proud of in them? What challenges assault the ministry that you do together?

15 Jesus Prays for Unity-John 17:20-26

Context: Jesus' prayer turns to others who would believe. He and the Father were one in mind and heart. He prayed that the believers would be so as well. He had already witnessed the disagreement of the disciples over who was the greatest. He knew that believers would have the same troubles.

Every parent loves to see their children get along. Yes, there may be squabbles from time to time, but we want our children to love each other so much that they would rally around each other if the chips were down. Jesus' children, the disciples, often squabbled among themselves who was the greatest. One pictures the rivalry among the twelve and the pained look on Jesus' face as He saw these men juggle for positions in an earthly kingdom that would never be. Thus, the prayer ends with a prayer for unity. Jesus wanted the disciples and all believers to be a close family who would stand by each other and support one another. He wanted them to love each other as the Father had loved Him.

Unity was important for the disciples because their message

would impact the young church in the book of Acts. "My prayer is not for them alone. I pray also for those who will believe in me through their message" (v.20) In a sense, every Christian has come to faith through the ministry and writings of the disciples. Some would write gospels and epistles. All of them would be instrumental in bringing the first generation of Christians to faith. Jesus wants all men to be one. He knows the divisions that will occur between Jew and Gentile. He knows the divisions that will occur in the early church. He prays for unity so that the church might not be divided by Satan.

Such unity is at the heart of the triune God. Our Lord is three persons, but He is one God. Father, Son, and Holy Spirit act together in the plan of salvation. The world cannot see our God, but they can see this truth about Him through His people. "that all of them may be one, Father, just as you are in me and I am in you. May they also be in us so that the world may believe that you have sent me." (v.21) People will learn about God by watching His people. The world mocks God when His church is divided and at each other's throats. Conversely, a church that loves and cares for each other draws people closer to God.

Yet unity is not just about getting along. It is not even about having the same doctrine. Unity comes when we love each other as if we were one. It is a unity that is only possible when Jesus lives in us and inspires us to love. "I in them and you in me. May they be brought to complete unity to let the world know that you sent me and have loved them even as you have loved me." (v.23) God is love and His love is infectious. Unity cannot be imposed by governments or programs. Unity comes from within as Jesus lives in us and inspires us to care about one another more than we care about ourselves. Those who have been to the cross of Jesus and seen His love for them are changed by our Lord. They will make sacrifices for each other and they will respond in love for strangers just because of the way that Jesus loves us.

The world around us is watching to see if we will love like Jesus or not. One of the things that most impresses the world is when Christians love each other. Someone has cancer and the congregation rallies around them bringing food, paying for medicine and visiting them often. A congregation has a fire at the church and the members pull together to rebuild God's home praising the Lord that no one was hurt. When the church is a family that cares about each other more than themselves, the world notices. The world cannot see our Lord, but they can have a sense of His love. The world can see that our God is different from all the other gods of the world. He is with His people and they are with each other in good times and in bad. What makes the church different is that our Lord is at the heart of every unified church. His love and sacrifice inspire us to be different. The unity that sets our God apart from other gods brings peace between members of the church family because everyone feels valued by our Lord. It is not a unity that the world imposes. It is a unity that flows from the forgiveness that we feel from God and the forgiveness and love that we have for each other. God gives us the opportunity to be and live with people who are different. He has made the Father known to us so that God's love may live in us and be made complete in us.

- Who do you feel distant from in the church? How

can you demonstrate God's love to them so that you

might become one?

16 Broken Sanctuary-Luke 22:39-48

Context: Jesus "went out as usual" to a quiet place where He could spend time praying before the arrest. The Garden of Gethsemane was on the Mount of Olives just east of Jerusalem and across from the temple. It was here that Jesus would draw strength from the Father.

A sanctuary is a quiet place where we can collect our thoughts and find a little peace. Sometimes sanctuary is a place. It may be a park bench or a porch swing. Sometimes it may be a relationship like a strong marriage or special friend. We feel relaxed and as if all is right with the world. Gethsemane must have been such a place. Jesus seems to have gone there often. It was the first place that the betrayer would look for Him that night. It was even on the way from Jerusalem to Bethany where Jesus and the disciples were staying during the Passover. What do you do when your sanctuary is broken? What do you do when life interferes with your peace or when that special relationship is broken? Come to Jesus and find calm when your sanctuary is gone. Learn from Jesus how to have sanctuary in chaos.

Jesus knew what was coming. The disciples may have walked to the garden feeling some of the joy of the Passover. Jesus had come to pray. "Father, if you are willing, take this cup from me; yet not my will, but yours be done." (v.42) He knows that Judas is already meeting with the Jews and that a mob will soon be assembled to take Him to the trials and ultimately the cross. He will be able to see their torches as they exit the eastern gate of Jerusalem, go down into the valley below and up the hill to the garden. The time of sanctuary is short. He must prepare for the chaos. Leaving the disciples at the edge of the garden, He begins to wrestle in prayer with what is coming.

Prayer is His ultimate sanctuary. The strength of this place is not its beauty or the earthy scents of the plants and soil. The strength of this place is the quiet He needs to spend time with the Father. Jesus is in torment. "And being in anguish, he prayed more earnestly, and his sweat was like drops of blood falling to the ground." (v.44). Luke shows the depth of His anguish in the garden. Sweat like drops of blood falls from His brow. He turns to the Father for help. He opens up a direct line to the heavens and seeks the help that only the Father can give. The world is about to explode around Jesus, but the Father is in control. He will pray three times this night. With every prayer, He lays His future and His whole being in the hands of the Father.

The suffering that Jesus would face over the next 24 hours could not be taken away. The cup of sorrow that was the cross was the means of salvation for all mankind. Jesus had to face it or mankind was doomed. Yet, the Father would not abandon the Son. He would strengthen Jesus for the task ahead. "An angel from heaven appeared to him and strengthened him." (v.43) Luke alone tells us of the Father's gift. The sorrowing Jesus was prepared so that He could confidently face the trials ahead. Leaving this place of prayer, He was ready to face Jew and Roman alike. He would even cause Pilate to be in awe of His calm demeanor. He would be ready to bring salvation to mankind even though He knew the cost.

As Jesus finished His prayer, He turned to the disciples. He knew of the temptation that they would face and the dangers that were all around them. He would protect them so that none of them would be lost that night. He will conquer their sin and give them life. He will become their sanctuary. Our earthly sanctuaries can all be broken, but our sanctuary with Jesus cannot be taken away. When we ask for His help in prayer He will always be there. When we find ourselves in danger, He will be our shield. Jesus has faced the dangers of life on our behalf and He will continue to watch over us and protect us if we will call to Him in prayer.

Jesus is our great helper and our peace. In the midst of the trials of life and the great unrest, we have a place of sanctuary. Our safe harbor is prayer with Jesus. As we find that quiet place where the noise is gone and we can concentrate on Jesus, we can lay all our troubles on Him. God may not always take the problems away. He may send an angel to give us strength just as He did Jesus in the garden. The important thing is that He will never abandon us. He will help us through each trial by guiding us and placing His power in our life. Sanctuary for us is not a place. It is a person. We find sanctuary and peace as we draw close to the one who faced danger and death for us.

- Where is your life exploding right now? What would you ask the Lord for in prayer that could bring some calm and peace to your life?

17 When Darkness Reigns-Luke 22:47-53

Context: A kiss is still a traditional greeting in many parts of the world, yet here it was used to show the mob which one was Jesus. It is the first sign that darkness will reign through the night. Only the resurrection will overcome the darkness. When you least expected it, a friend stabbed you in the back. You were working on a project together and they left you hanging or even blamed you for the failure of the project. Life had seemed so good and then evil brought in darkness. It happens to all of us from time to time. Sometimes, we can even see it coming or are warned by someone else. Despite all of Jesus' warnings at the last supper table, the disciples were truly unprepared for the challenges in the Garden of Gethsemane. Jesus had told them to pray and all they could do was sleep. Evil will attack people whether they are ready or not. The question is what we will do when we are unfairly attacked.

Having left the last supper, Judas goes to rally the troops and bring them to Gethsemane where he believed Jesus would be.

What should have been a sign of tenderness was given as a sign to the Jewish leaders in the darkness of Gethsemane as to whom they should arrest. Jesus sees right through the betrayal. "Jesus asked him, Judas, are you betraying the Son of Man with a kiss?" (v.48) The kiss is the kiss of the hypocrite. The gesture of greeting is one of betrayal. One of the twelve who had been with Jesus for years leads the enemy to arrest Him. He had seen Jesus walk through crowds who wanted to kill him (Luke 4:30) and walk on water. Did he think that he could arrest the one that could "call down legions of angels" if Jesus was not willing to die?

The attack was also cowardly. Jesus points out why they had come at night. "Every day I was with you in the temple courts, and you did not lay a hand on me. But this is your hour--when darkness reigns."(v.53) The leaders were afraid to arrest Jesus in the midst of all the people who would see His capture and who might revolt. Here in the darkness, they could come while those who had praised Jesus on Palm Sunday were asleep. They would rush through the trial and have Jesus on a cross before the people even noticed. It was cowardly. Instead of making their case and showing that Jesus was evil, they worked in Satan's time of darkness because their actions could not stand the light of day.

Jesus called the disciples to rise, but it may have been the light of the torches and the noise of the mob that finally woke them up. When they saw what was happening, they reacted. And one of them struck the servant of the high priest, cutting off his right ear. (v.50) The gospel of John tells us that the one who cut off the servant's ear was Peter. His reaction is what we often do when we find ourselves threatened. He reacted with equal force to the evil that he was experienced. It is easy to do harm to those who threaten to do harm to us. He had boasted that he was willing to die with Jesus back in the upper room. As one man with a sword fighting against a small army who had come to arrest Jesus, he was about to make that boast a reality.

Peter may have thought that it was time to fight, but Jesus put a stop to it. He reacted to the evil of the mob with a miracle of kindness. "But Jesus answered, "No more of this!" And he touched the man's ear and healed him." (v.51) Even as the mob prepared to lead Jesus off to trial and to the cross, Jesus would first stop to care for one of His enemies. In showing kindness, he repaired the harm that Peter had done so that Peter could not be arrested or tried. He showed His true nature of love and kindness even as the mob was showing their evil and cowardice. It was not a flashy miracle and I am sure that many of Jewish leaders would deny that it even happened. Yet, Jesus battled evil with kindness and trusted the Father in this dark hour.

Each of us will face times of betrayal and cowardly enemies in our lifetime. We have to decide how we will react when we are attacked. Will we stoop to their level and lash out like Peter did or will we show kindness to others at a time when they least expect it? Jesus shows us how to be in control of the situation. To strike out continues the cycle of revenge and hurt. To show kindness leaves our hands clean and allows the Heavenly Father to bring His justice. There are times we need to defend ourselves with a lawyer or the court, but we need to do that in full light and transparency so that justice is truly done. To strike back and create our own justice in the darkness of evil is to enter the realm of Satan and not to let the Lord be in control.

- Who has hurt you recently? How might you respond with kindness? How might that heal your hurt and repair the relationship?

18 Don't Give In To Evil-Mark 14:53-65

Context: From Gethsemane, Jesus was taken to the home of Caiaphas, the High Priest, after making a stop at the home of Annas, the former High Priest (John 18). Here, the group would gather evidence for the trial before the full Sanhedrin. Evil is all around us. It is a politician slinging dirt about a rival. It is a competitor who undercuts us in business. Our natural response is to be as crafty and mean-spirited as they are. We want to fight back by picketing a business or suing "the pants off" someone who has done us wrong. We forget that Satan's aim is to make good people just as evil as the world in which they live. He wants to bring us down to the level of those who hurt us. He wants us to become evil. The way to fight evil is not by being evil, but by being good in the face of evil. In His trial, Jesus followed this simple principle: When surrounded by evil, don't give in. He never became evil like those who wanted Him dead.

Sadly, you can expect evil to play dirty. On the night before His crucifixion, Jesus did not get a fair trial. The outcome of the trial was determined long before the Sanhedrin had gathered. The problem was that Jesus was so good and holy that they were having trouble convicting Him. "The chief priests and the whole Sanhedrin were looking for evidence against Jesus so that they could put him to death, but they did not find any." (v.55) Jewish law required that two witnesses come forward and agree on their testimony if a man was to be found guilty. Many falsely testified against Jesus, but the Sanhedrin could not find two witnesses that could agree. If they couldn't find witnesses, the Sanhedrin would not be able to condemn Jesus under the "cloak" of justice. Evil would have to show itself for what it really was.

Usually, a person facing death will try to justify what they did. They will argue with witnesses and protest that they were innocent. Jesus kept quiet. The silence of Jesus must have been unnerving for the High Priest. "Then the high priest stood up before them and asked Jesus, "Are you not going to answer? What is this testimony that these men are bringing against you?" (v.60) Jesus had the luxury of keeping quiet and letting evil destroy itself. The false testimonies could not agree. No charge was going to stick. He had led a holy life healing the sick and teaching people about the Father. Jesus would not respond evil for evil. He would not panic. His silence spoke volumes about His innocence.

The high priest, sensing that the trial is falling apart, does the unthinkable. He calls on Jesus to incriminate Himself by asking "Are you the Christ, the Son of the Blessed One?" (v.61). Jesus is under solemn oath and must answer. He knows that the answer will seal His fate. Yet, He will no longer keep silent. He must tell the truth even if it condemns Him. "I am," said Jesus. "And you will see the Son of Man sitting at the right hand of the Mighty One and coming on the clouds of heaven." (v.62) To keep quiet when asked if He was the Christ might make it seem like this statement was just as false as the ones that came before it. Jesus boldly tells the truth invoking the Holy name of God, "I am". He proclaims that the Jewish leaders will see the truth that they have refused to acknowledge when Jesus comes to judge them all.

Jesus would have us give away worldly things so that we do not give away the heavenly things. Give away your money or your property rather than ruining your reputation. Let someone have the seat of power rather than scheming and you will show the ones who are evil or unworthy. You have a character and values that you have been given by God at a great price. Do not let evil bring you down to its level. Respond in love and let evil fall apart on its own. Live a life filled with love and mercy like Jesus so that people have difficulty finding a charge against you. People will remember your kindness and your honesty as evil shows itself for what it is. Good defeats evil. More evil for evil brings down everyone involved.

Instead of fighting evil, trust God to save you from evil. Jesus' answer to Caiaphas is telling. "And you will see the Son of Man sitting at the right hand of the Mighty One and coming on the clouds of heaven." (v.62) Evil may think it has won, but God will triumph in the end. Everyone who condemned Jesus will face terror when they are judged on the last day by the Messiah who stands before them. God does judge evil in the proper time. Rather than becoming evil to fight evil, we would do well to live our lives in the purity and honesty of God. Let the Lord deal with those who would hurt us. We may face hardship at the hands of evil, but we need to be confident that the Lord protects His people.

- Who do you often find yourself angry with? How does your anger make things worse? What could you do to bring peace and kindness to this relationship?

19 Preparing for Temptation-Matthew 26:69-75

Context: Peter and another disciple (John) had both followed Jesus to Caiaphas's home. The other disciple was known to the high priest and allowed inside. Peter stood in the courtyard by himself hearing the trial inside.

Most of us know how to pack for a vacation. We make lists of what we need to do from getting plane tickets to packing the swim suits. We often bring more clothes that we could possible wear just because we don't know what the weather will be like. So, why do we face Satan's temptations unprepared? Why do we just go and "wing" it in life as we face coworkers who test our patience or a short skirt that catches our eyes? We know that we will face the pull of sin every day of our lives. We have our default ways of dealing with temptations that seldom work. We get mad at ourselves when we fall to sin and have to pay the price in broken relationships and broken character. Simon Peter forgot a simple rule that we all need to apply. When we walk through life without Christ, we will fall into temptation.

As Peter faces the lure of sin, we see three common answers to dealing with troublesome situations. The first solution is often to try to ignore it and hope that it goes away. "But he denied it before them all." I don't know what you're talking about," he said." (v. 70) The servant girl sees Peter and asks a question. Her question may have been an accusation or simply innocent chatter. Either way, it alarms Peter. Jesus is on trial and one would imagine that Peter in the courtyard can hear the shouting and the allegations against Jesus. Peter is afraid that he may be put on trial as well. He brushes off the question pretending that a simple denial will settle the matter. He moves from the fire and the light into the shadows hoping that people will forget him (v.71).

Peter may move away, but that doesn't stop the discussion. Another girl sees Peter. It may have been the girl who let John and Peter come into the courtyard. She looks at him and picks up the discussion stating plainly that Peter was one of those who were with Jesus. Peter's answer gets a little stronger. "He denied it again, with an oath: "I don't know the man!" (v.72) Not only does Peter deny knowing Jesus, but he swears that what he is saying is true. A simple denial didn't work and so Peter swears to a bald faced lie hoping that this is the end of it. He begins to feel like things are closing in on him.

After a little while, Peter becomes the center of the discussion around the fire. One of the people gets the nerve to confront Peter and declare that Peter must be one of the followers of Jesus since he has a Galilean accent. John's gospel says that this man saw Peter earlier in the Garden of Gethsemane. Now Peter is really scared. His final solution is filled with emotion. "Then he began to call down curses on himself and he swore to them, "I don't know the man!" Immediately a rooster crowed." (v.74) The lies have not worked and so he starts to curse like a mad man. Perhaps he was hoping that people would back away from him the way that you back away from a lunatic. Ironically, Peter's actions confirm their suspicions. His actions prove he was with Jesus.

Peter hears the cock crow and it all comes back to him. "Then Peter remembered the word Jesus had spoken: "Before the rooster crows, you will disown me three times." And he went outside and wept bitterly." (v.75) He breaks down and leaves the place of temptation weeping bitterly because he had let Jesus down. When we fail, repentance is the only Godly solution. It is the difference between Peter and Judas. Peter repented. Judas tried to fix his sin. Like Peter, we can't justify the sin; we have to throw ourselves on the mercy of Jesus and His forgiveness. We can't just pretend that it didn't happen and there is no way we can fix it. Forgiveness is the only way to stop the damage and begin the healing. Jesus will strengthen us and help us to fight temptation when it comes again.

Is there a way to prepare for temptation so that we are able to fight Satan's attacks? There was for Peter. In the Garden of Gethsemane, Jesus had asked the disciples to pray so that they would not fall into temptation. (Matt. 26:41). One wonders if Peter would have so easily given into temptation if he had prayed for hours like Jesus. Prayer and time in God's word will not guarantee that we avoid every sin, but it will cut down on the number of times that Satan defeats us. In prayer and Bible study, we connect with Jesus so that He is part of our daily lives. His wisdom will help us see the temptations and His power will help us overcome them. We cannot battle Satan

alone. We need Jesus to battle our temptations for us.

- What struggles are you facing right now in your

walk with Christ? What help would you ask for in

prayer?

20 Undoing Our Wrongs-Matthew 27:1-10

Context: Judas' motives in agreeing to betray Jesus are hard to understand. The sight of Jesus' arrest, however, unnerves Judas and he returns to the chief priests to undo what he has done. He wants to fix what he has done.

"Why did I do that? I knew that it was wrong and that it would only get me into trouble." Everyone has times where you do or say something that you wish you could take back. You may know you sinned right away or it might take a little while for the words or actions to explode and cause you trouble. Now, what do you do? You could try to make things right if that is possible. You can apologize to the person who you hurt, but that may not be accepted. Can anything take away the guilt that you feel and allow you to move on with your life? I know of only one thing that can take away the guilt so that you can begin to repair the damage. This is the story of someone close to Jesus who never knew such forgiveness.

In order to make things look more legitimate, the Sanhedrin had another trial in the morning. Perhaps Judas was nearby.

He saw that Jesus was condemned and was seized with remorse. "I have sinned," he said, "for I have betrayed innocent blood." (v.4a) What he had done finally dawned on him. Perhaps he had handed Jesus over to spur the Master into using His great power to create an earthly kingdom. Perhaps he was now having second thoughts about deserting his Lord and friend. We will never know. His remorse seems to lead him to despair. What would he do next? Things had not worked out like he had wanted them to. How would he make things right?

Judas began by trying to undo what he had done. "When Judas, who had betrayed him, saw that Jesus was condemned, he was seized with remorse and returned the thirty silver coins to the chief priests and the elders." (v.3) Sadly, it was too late. Jesus had been found guilty and was bound for trial with Pilate. The chief priests could not undo what had happened. They had no reason to even try. They had wanted Jesus put to death. They had looked for false evidence and interrupted their Passover preparations when Judas had presented the opportunity to arrest Jesus quietly.

Like many others, Judas could not undo the actions that he had taken. Things were too advanced and the people he had bargained with were so evil that they didn't care about his guilt.

Their reply shows how little they cared. "What is that to us?" they replied. "That's your responsibility." (v.4b) The religious leaders would offer no forgiveness for Judas' sin. What is done is done. Judas is left with his guilt and sees no future. He hangs himself as a way out of the pain and responsibility for betraying his Lord. Oddly, the priests have their own guilt to deal with. They have to decide what to do with the "blood money" since it cannot go back into God's treasury. They decide to ease their conscience by using it for a charity. They would buy a field where foreigners could be buried if they died while visiting Jerusalem. It would not take away their guilt, but it might ease their consciences.

Neither Judas nor the priests could undo their sin. Jesus was bound and on His way to Pilate and the cross. What they had done would be forever held against them. Such is our fear. Lies cannot be taken back. Sinful actions seem to doom us with painful consequences. Yet, what is impossible for us is possible for Jesus. We cannot undo the sin, yet Jesus can pardon our transgression. As we confess our sin, He is faithful and promises to forgive. He has paid for our sin on the cross and will wipe it away. He will also help us to learn what we can do to deal with the consequences of our sin. Our times of prayer and study of His word are times that help us repair our lives and chart a course for the future. He alone can wipe away the sin and help us repair the damage.

I would like to imagine that the story could have had a different ending. Imagine Judas crying through the night like Peter did instead of taking his life. On Easter, he could have heard the stories of Jesus' resurrection like the Peter did. What would Jesus' response have been if Judas had sought Him out? I feel confident that Jesus would have forgiven him and restored him just like Peter. Our Lord is always more willing to forgive than we are to ask. When we sin what seems an unforgivable sin, we need to come to Jesus. You and I will be forgiven if we approach HIm and repent. Whenever we sin, the real solution begins by coming to Jesus and asking for forgiveness. Jesus can undo what we have done by the power of the cross.

- Which was more damaging for Judas – to deny Jesus or to not seek forgiveness? What keeps you from bringing your deep dark secrets to the Lord for healing?

21 Looking For Loopholes-Luke 23:1-25

Context: Early in the morning, Jesus is brought to Pilate by the Jews. Pilate was the Roman governor and could pronounce the death sentence the Jews were seeking. Pilate becomes convinced that Jesus is not guilty. One wonders if he feared the crowds who had followed Jesus as well as the leaders who were before him.

Many people look for loopholes when they are caught with hard decisions. "It is okay for us to live together since we plan to get married." "I know that I lied, but he was telling lies, too." We act as if there are times that it is acceptable to do what we know is wrong. We create loopholes to make sin look more acceptable to ourselves and to others. It doesn't change the consequences. Our lie may get us in trouble whether others are lying as well or not. Their sin doesn't make it right. The guilt still hangs over us and we often feel guilty in spite of the loophole that we tried to create. In the passion story of Jesus, one man tries to find a loophole out of a painful decision. Despite his attempts to look innocent, the guilt of what he did still remains. The church, to this day, still speaks of his sin in our creeds.

Pilate enters the story of Jesus as the Roman governor who must try Jesus on behalf of the people. The Jews want Jesus dead but cannot pronounce that sentence for themselves. They bring civil charges against Jesus to force Pilate into having Jesus crucified. Pilate is not a fool, however. He interrogates Jesus about His kingship and quickly concludes that Jesus has committed no crime. "Then Pilate announced to the chief priests and the crowd, "I find no basis for a charge against this man." (v.4) His decision is met with cries from the angry mob. Always the politician, Pilate looks for the way out. How can he release this innocent Jesus without causing a riot that will threaten his future?

The first loophole that Pilate uses is to send Jesus on to someone else. "When he learned that Jesus was under Herod's jurisdiction, he sent him to Herod, who was also in Jerusalem at that time." (v.7) Jesus was Galilean and Pilate saw the opportunity to get Jesus off his hands. He sent Jesus off to Herod Antipas who was the ruler of Galilee. Pilate wanted Herod to judge Jesus so that when Jesus was declared innocent or guilty, no one could blame him. Herod asked Jesus questions and had some fun mocking Him, but Herod could find no guilt in Jesus. Instead of setting Jesus free as Pilate had hoped, he just sent Jesus back to Pilate. Pilate would still have to make the final decision after all. His plan had not worked.

Pilate then tried to make Jesus look good. He brought out a murderer named Barabbas. He had Jesus beaten by his soldiers. Surely, that would satisfy the Jews. "Wanting to release Jesus, Pilate appealed to them again. But they kept shouting, "Crucify him! Crucify him!" (v.20-21) Pilate appealed to them and tried to bargain with them, but nothing worked. He could see that he was losing the battle and that the Emperor would blame him for the riot. He did what any good politician would do. He washed his hands of Jesus and let the crowd have what they wanted. Jesus would go to the cross even though Pilate knew that our Savior was innocent. He could salve his conscience knowing that he had saved himself by sacrificing Jesus.

Today Pilate is remembered as the one who had Jesus crucified. He knew Jesus was innocent but was more concerned with his position than his character. It is still easy to want to take the easy way out when we find ourselves called upon to do something difficult or take a tough stance. It may help us in the short term, but often our lies are discovered or people see through our weak character. We may be remembered for years for what we did. God wants us to take the hard road and He promises to be with those who live with Godly values and character. God knows that what we do today affects tomorrow. The easy way out is often the way that leads to disaster.

"Everyone else is doing it!" is a common cry. Yet that loophole doesn't make it right or take away the consequences of a person's sin. Suppose that everyone lied as a first defense. Suppose that everyone decided that it was okay to let their anger turn to violence. Would you want to live in that world? Someone has to stand up for truth and it should be us. Yes, it is hard to admit we were wrong. It can be hard to turn the other cheek when someone hurts you. We need to remember that loopholes didn't work for Pilate and they won't work for us.

What brings lasting success is to live with God's character and

values. You will have a legacy of being someone of character

and trustworthiness. We are the way that the world sees

God's truth and sees that God's ways actually do work.

- Why aren't loopholes successful in the long run?

  What are you telling yourself about your life that you

  know is not true?

22 Is He Your King?-Mark 15:1-15

Context: When Jesus returns from an audience with Herod, Pilate must make a decision concerning Jesus' fate. He knows that Jesus is innocent and wants to release Him. Instead, he gives into the crowd and sends Jesus off to die.

More people used to fill our churches and worship Jesus. No one worked on Sunday except the policemen, firemen, and those at the hospital. Television was sanitized of swearing and nudity. Christian values were everywhere and many who didn't go to church accepted that the Ten Commandments taught the difference between right and wrong. It isn't that way anymore. Few want to follow Jesus. Other gods and things have pushed Jesus to the side. It is not uncommon to see a church half empty on any given Sunday. Other things are crowned as "king" in our life. Jesus gets the leftovers of time and resources. In the text, Pilate is faced with the charge that Jesus is king. Pilate must decide whether to accept or reject the royalty of Jesus. All of us must choose to follow Jesus as our leader or follow the ways of the world. Only one can be in charge of your life.

The choice is not always easy. Jesus will not play games, but wants us to freely make the choice to follow Him. Pilate can see that Jesus is innocent, but he wants Jesus to persuade him. "So again Pilate asked him, "Aren't you going to answer? See how many things they are accusing you of." (v.4) Pilate may have heard how easily Jesus had countered the arguments of the Pharisees throughout His ministry. Yet, Jesus does not cooperate with Pilate. He shows that He is in charge by letting His silence expose the hatred and lies of the priests. He regally stood silent and in control as the rest of the world fell apart and incriminated itself. As king, Jesus didn't need to defend himself. Pilate only needed to do what he already knew was right.

Having failed to get Jesus to defend himself, Pilate tries to make Jesus look innocent. He brings out a notorious criminal called Jesus Barabbas who had murdered people in an uprising. The choice is simple – Jesus the murderer who rules by hate or King Jesus the healer who rules by love. Surely, the crowd will want Jesus when He is compared to such a person as this. Yet, they don't. "But the chief priests stirred up the crowd to have Pilate release Barabbas instead." (v.11) Pilate's ploy to save Jesus doesn't work. You can't put a spin on Jesus and make Him palatable to those who hate Him and want no part of following Him. Stirred up by the chief priests who are filled with hate, the crowds demand that King Jesus be put to death.

When it was obvious that the crowd wanted no part of Jesus and His kingdom, Pilate quickly bows to their demands. "Wanting to satisfy the crowd, Pilate released Barabbas to them. He had Jesus flogged, and handed him over to be crucified." (v.15) Pilate had him beaten because the King had not satisfied him or the crowds. Pilate had no king but Caesar. He had no king but the king of self-preservation. A weak king like Jesus could easily be disposed of. Nothing was lost. Let the sign on His cross mock Jesus and the Jews by calling Him king. Pilate would show the Jews what he thought of their king. The Jewish King would die like the rest of those who opposed Rome.

Pilate knew that Jesus was innocent, but he never understood how Jesus could be a king. The crowd which should have adored Jesus hated Him and refused to follow Him. Jesus still presents every human a choice. Will you follow me or will you have your own king? Around us, there will be many in our schools or workplace that malign Jesus and cast Him aside. We don't need to argue with them. Simply tell people how much Jesus has blessed our lives and that Jesus desires to bless them as well. Let them know the joy of being in His kingdom. Let people see the impact that Jesus has had on our lives, our marriage, and our character. Admittedly, not everyone will listen, but many will find it hard to argue when they see the blessings that happen in your life because you follow Jesus as your Lord.

Could Jesus have forced Pilate to free him? Surely things would have been different if Jesus had called just two angels to stand on either side of Him that early morning. No one would have laid a hand on Him. Jesus could still force people to make Him their king. He could cause something bad to happen to you every time you miss church or lie more than once in a day. He could make you obey Him out of fear of punishment. Yet, God doesn't work that way. He wants you to choose Him as your king freely. He wants people to love Him and want to be His children. He never seeks slaves who are forced into His kingdom. Just remember that you do have to make a choice. You must choose between Jesus and the world, you can't have both.

- What shows people that Jesus is the king of your life? What blessings do you and other Christians have because you are part of His kingdom?

23 A Cross of Hope-Mark 15:21-37

Context: Having been found guilty by Pilate, Jesus was led to the cross around 9 AM. Because of the beatings that He had faced at the hands of the Jews and the Romans, Jesus had little strength to carry the cross. The situation looked hopeless. In writing to the Romans, Mark only spoke a few words. "And they crucified him" (v.24). He did not have to explain the process of crucifixion or its pain. Every Roman citizen knew exactly what crucifixion was. Many had seen it with their own eyes. If the cross was well understood in Roman times, I think it is poorly understood in our times. Millions of people wear crosses as jewelry without a single thought of what the cross really means. Would they wear a medallion of a hangman's noose or electric chair so casually? What is the cross about? Is it only comfort for life after death or is there comfort in the cross for this life as well. Come with me to the cross and see a Savior who you can identify with and who will help you in those hopeless moments of life.

Jesus understands when you feel too weak to go on. Every

condemned man was to carry the crossbeam of his cross through the streets to the place of execution. Jesus was too weak to carry His cross. They had beaten Him till He was bloody and half dead as part of the trial. He could barely stumble to the cross. They had to grab a man off the street to carry His cross for Him. "A certain man from Cyrene, Simon, the father of Alexander and Rufus, was passing by on his way in from the country, and they forced him to carry the cross." (v.21) Jesus couldn't manage the weight of the cross by Himself. He needed help. We forget how they abused Him and how they tortured His poor body and robbed it of all its natural strength. As you look at the cross, know that He understands your pain because He has felt pain himself.

He knows what it is to be kicked when you are down. It wasn't enough for the Jews and their leaders to bring Him to Pilate to crucify Him; they had to humiliate Him on the cross. "Those who passed by hurled insults at him, shaking their heads and saying, "So! You who are going to destroy the temple and build it in three days" (v.29) They mocked His promises of salvation and renewal. They mocked His miracles and made them look simple. Here are the religious leaders who should have been defending their Savior ridiculing Jesus for all the help that He had given to others. All His kind deeds of healing the sick and raising the dead were being thrown back in His face. As you look at the cross, know that He understands. He has been mocked worse than any of us.

He also knows what it feels like to be all alone. Six hours on the cross surrounded by hecklers without His friends to support Him. Only His mother and John showed up at the cross to comfort Him and He is unable to help His mother in her pain. All the other disciples are gone. All the people who He healed are gone. Even God has abandoned Him. He cries out the words from Psalm 22. "And at the ninth hour Jesus cried out in a loud voice, "Eloi, Eloi, lama sabachthani?"-- which means, "My God, my God, why have you forsaken me?" (v.34) He is separated from God because of our sin. He must suffer sin's penalty of hell on the cross. As you look at the cross, know that He understands. He knows how vulnerable you feel. He knows how sometimes we feel when there is no one to support or help us.

We often avoid thinking about the cross because it is painful to see Jesus suffer. We may even feel guilty that He had to suffer for us. Yet, when darkness comes in our life, the cross is where we should go for help. There we will find one who has been weak, humiliated and alone like we have been. There we will find one who is able to give forgiveness and love in His pain. There we will find the comfort that we need because He understands and has triumphed over the darkness. When we come and touch Him on that cross, we find healing for our emotions and problems now as well as the salvation of heaven. Comfort and peace come when you lay all your fears and guilt at the cross. You know that He understands and that He can help us.

When you are hopeless, come to the king. The Roman cross was meant to symbolize the power of the Roman government. It showed that Caesar was in charge. Jesus' cross, however, shows the power of our God. That is why it has become the symbol of the church. It shows the forgiveness that comes because Jesus died for us and for our sins. No other religion in the world has a God who understands human pain and suffering. No other religion has the answer for weakness, humiliation, and loneliness. Jesus has experienced all of those and conquered them. He has been on the cross and He says that He understands and He will help. When you find yourself dealing with the darkness of the world, there is only one place to go. You go to the cross. There you will find the help you need.

- What pain do you need to bring to the cross? What aspect of Jesus' suffering demonstrates that He really understands your pain?

24 Forsaken-Matt. 27:32-50

Context: Jesus hung on the cross from the 3rd hour (9 AM) to the 9th hour (3 PM). At noon, the sky became dark and Jesus spoke of His loneliness and His confidence in the Father. Imagine yourself sitting in the dark crying as your heart aches. You have had a big argument with your parents or your spouse. You suddenly feel like you don't have a friend in the world. No one loves you. No one understands what you are feeling or is willing to take your side. Thoughts of anger and hatred rage through your mind even though you know that such thoughts are wrong and harmful. Who can you go to? Who will listen to you as you pour out your heart? The answer is Jesus. He will listen to you because He, too, has been all alone. He will help you find the answers. He understands what you are feeling. We often forget how lonely it must have been on the cross. At His greatest time of need, Jesus didn't seem to have a friend in the world.

The twelve had been His friends for years. Where were they now? Jesus had been through trials and had been publically beaten. He was so weary and weak that He couldn't even carry His own cross. Surely, Peter or John was nearby and would gladly help their savior with His cross. No, His disciples were gone and many were hiding. A stranger was forced to help. "As they were going out, they met a man from Cyrene, named Simon, and they forced him to carry the cross." (v.32) Jesus had shown His love to the disciples by washing their feet. In His greatest hour of weakness, it was a stranger who would be forced to help because His disciples and all those He had healed and taught were gone. Jesus was all alone. The crowds had cheered His arrival into Jerusalem on Palm Sunday. They had cheered Him as the Son of David and remembered all the miraculous things that He had done. Hanging on a cross on Good Friday, Jesus gets no respect. "Those who passed by hurled insults at him, shaking their heads and saying, "You who are going to destroy the temple and build it in three days, save yourself!"(v.39-40) Those passing by still remember His ministry, but they throw it up in His face. You expect the Pharisees and Sadducees who worked so hard to crucify Him to mock Him. Yet, where are the words of comfort or compassion from those He had healed or taught? No one takes up His cause or gives Him respect. Jesus was all alone.

Recalling the words of David in Psalm 22, Jesus cries out, "My God, my God, why have you forsaken me?" (v.46) These are the words of one who is used to having the Father as a constant companion. David cried them out in the psalm as he wondered why God didn't answer him in his time of need. Jesus cries them because, for the first time, the Father didn't have His back. Darkness is over the world and during that time of darkness, Jesus bore the sins of the world (2 Cor. 5:21). God turned His back on Jesus as He carried those sins because God could not look with favor on one with the sins of the world. Our sin separated Jesus from the Father. The Father abandoned Jesus so that the penalty for sin could be complete. Jesus was all alone.

Jesus was forsaken so that we would never have to be forsaken by God. He was forsaken so that our sins could be paid for. We will sin throughout our life, but the cross of Jesus means that God will always forgive us and draw us close when we repent. Jesus was forsaken so that we might have the promise of eternal life with God. The resurrection sealed God's offer to always be with us. Matthew 28:20 makes the promise that no matter where we are, God will be there to listen to us and to help us. We never have to be alone for we have God on our side and can call our loving Heavenly Father at any time and in any place.

In the darkness, when no one seems to care, know that Jesus understands exactly how you feel. He was alone in a way that none of us will ever have to be. Reach out to Him. Instead of pouting, you can pray. Tell Jesus all the things that you are feeling. Let Him help you sort out your feelings and figure out what you can do next. Instead of stewing in anger, you can study His word. Let Jesus comfort you and help you see that you are not alone. Let Him share a Bible story or words of guidance so that you don't make matters worse. In those lonely times, we should seek out the one person who will never abandon us. Seek out Jesus so that you can talk to Him in prayer and hear His advice in the word. Jesus was all alone. You and I need never be alone for we have Jesus.

- Think of a time when you were all alone. How do you think that Jesus felt on the cross? What would it mean for you that Jesus will always listen?

25 Forgiveness Changes Lives-Luke 23:32-49

Context: Luke and John each record three different words of Jesus from the cross. The first two words recorded in Luke are both about forgiveness. The third word of Jesus in Luke brings a response from Roman and Jew alike that is not recorded in the other gospels.

You thought it, but you never said it. A friend gossiped about you. Your spouse spent a lot of money without asking your input. You forgave them both, but you never told them that you forgave them. It doesn't matter, does it? The truth is that a spoken word of forgiveness has a lot of power. You may have forgiven them in your heart, but they are still living with the guilt. You may have forgiven them, but they are not sure how to act around you. When forgiveness is spoken, it has the power to change lives and to rebuild relationships. It can be a lot of work to take the time to forgive someone, but the effect that a word of forgiveness can have is powerful. In Luke's account of the crucifixion, we see the power of forgiveness first hand. Forgiveness can change lives.

Only in Luke, do we have Jesus' words of forgiveness as the Romans are nailing Him to the cross. "Jesus said, "Father, forgive them, for they do not know what they are doing." (v.34) His first words from the cross were about others. Instead of calling down curses on those who crucified an innocent man, Jesus reaches out with love and forgiveness. He was dying for them and for the rest of the world. All of us who sin put Him on the cross just as much as the Romans and the Jews. Jesus wanted His suffering and death to be for our benefit and not to our detriment. He publicly asks the Father to forgive and shows by His words and His actions that He does not hate them for what they are doing.

One of the thieves begins his crucifixion mocking Jesus like the others (Mt. 27:44), but the words and actions of Jesus have an effect on him. Luke alone records his request. "Jesus, remember me when you come into your kingdom." (v.42) It is a plea for grace. This thief had the courage to break from the crowd and trust the dying king. He took the words nailed above Jesus' head and the forgiving nature of our Lord to heart and made the astonishing request. Jesus' reply is just as remarkable. He forgave the thief and promised him the gift of salvation that could only come because of the mercy of the cross. The life of the thief was finished, but again Jesus spoke mercy and forgiveness and the man could die in peace.

Matthew and Mark record some of the words of the centurion in their gospels, but Luke alone records his praise of God and the righteousness of Jesus. "The centurion, seeing what had happened, praised God and said, "Surely this was a righteous man." (v.47) The centurion understood like Pilate had, that Jesus was innocent and did not deserve to die. He had been impressed with the dignity, courage, and words of forgiveness that he had heard from Jesus. Jesus had not stooped to condemn this centurion or the others with him who had crucified Him. He had shown that He was a righteous man by his mercy for the thief and the kindness He had shown to those who had hurt Him. He had forgiven and was more righteous than anyone else there at the cross.

Luke alone shares the reaction of the crowd to the death of Jesus. "When all the people who had gathered to witness this sight saw what took place, they beat their breasts and went away." (v.48) Many had come to condemn and ridicule Him. Others may have just stopped as they passed the cross on their way into town. Those who gathered were so touched by His death that they beat their breasts. The forgiveness of the cross shows the heart of our God. Jesus turned the other cheek and people left knowing that they were in the presence of someone greater than they. As we forgive others, we have a chance to show people a side of God that many do not expect. Our God is powerful, but He is also loving and forgiving as well.

Forgiving people in your heart will release you from the pull of revenge or anger. Forgiving others with your lips will take away the guilt and blame that weighs them down. It will rebuild relationships that have been damaged by sin and strengthen friendships with the power of our forgiving God. When we forgive as Jesus did from the cross, others will hear the power of God's love and some will be changed like the thief. Others will have their views challenged like the crowd and the centurion. People will see a new side of our God by the forgiveness we share. They will see the love of Jesus from the cross is for them as well. When someone has hurt you, forgive them. Forgive them in your heart, but also forgive them verbally so that they can have the benefit of forgiveness as well.

- Who do you need to give the words of forgiveness to in your life? How has the forgiveness of one you care about lifted your guilt and healed the relationship?

26 Suffering Alone?-John 19:16-30

Context: John is the only disciple to be an eyewitness the suffering of Jesus on the cross. His gospel contrasts the callous fight over Jesus between Pilate and the Jews with the love of a mother and Jesus' closest disciple.

"I hurt all over and no one seems to care!" You sit alone in a hospital room with a dying spouse or child. You have just lost your job and security stands over you as you clean out your desk. No one seems to care about you. No one says even a simple word of comfort or that they are sorry for what is happening to you. You want to lash out in anger at the people who seem to be so callous. You want to scream at God that He should do something to help you in your pain. What will you do next? Is there anyone who understands what you are going through? Is there anyone who cares about your pain and your sorrow? Yes, you and I will never be alone because there is someone who understands and will always listen and help. His name is Jesus. He knows what it is like when so many don't care about you.

Pilate sacrificed Jesus to save himself. Now Pilate uses the death of Jesus to get back at the Jews who had forced him to kill an innocent man. It was required that the criminal wears a placard announcing his crime. Pilate had put the charge against Jesus in three languages so that everyone could see the crime the Jews accused Him of. Yet, it riled the Jews. "The chief priests of the Jews protested to Pilate, "Do not write 'The King of the Jews,' but that this man claimed to be king of the Jews." (v.21) Pilate knew that the charge would insult and embarrass the Jews for it showed how Rome would deal with anyone who opposed it. Instead of caring about Jesus and protecting the innocent man, Pilate used Jesus as a weapon against the Jews who had forced his hand. He used Jesus to mock them publicly.

The soldiers were present for the six hours of Jesus' suffering on the cross. It was their job to be there and to make sure that no one interfered with the sentence. The soldiers were so used to the suffering of the crucifixion that they didn't even notice Jesus' pain. They focused on the spoils rather than the person. "When the soldiers crucified Jesus, they took his

clothes, dividing them into four shares, one for each of them"
(v.23) It didn't matter whether Jesus' sentence was fair. What
mattered to the soldiers was that each got a fair share of the
spoils. They ignored His suffering while they sought their own
gain. His clothes were split equally, and the men gambled for
the one piece that could not be divided.

Finally, we see a few who care, but who cannot help Him.
Horrified by the gruesome scene, they seem to have no words
of comfort to give. Surely, if anyone could have comforted
Jesus, it would have been His mother and the beloved
disciple. Yet, it is Jesus who will reach out to them in their
suffering and care for their needs. "When Jesus saw his
mother there, and the disciple whom he loved standing
nearby, he said to his mother, "Dear woman, here is your
son," (v.26) The Son gave His mother to His friend that they
both might comfort one another in the days ahead. The
adopted mother and son were still together as they waited for
Pentecost (Acts 1:14). Jesus in His pain showed love to those
suffering around Him.

He suffered in a way that we don't ever have to experience.

He suffered alone. The great joy for us is that we are not in the hospital room alone. Jesus is there. We don't clean out the desk when we are fired or face any other kind of disappointment alone. Jesus is there, too. Jesus may have been forsaken by the Father (Matt. 27:46), but He will never forsake us. He understands what it is to suffer. He understands what it is to feel all alone. He has been there. He feels your pain and He answers when you call in prayer. Like John and Mary at the cross, we find that the one who suffered reaches out to us to give us His comfort and support. He will not let us down. He will be there even at the times when we don't see Him or feel His presence.

When you feel all alone, it is time to pray. It is time to seek the comfort and understanding of your suffering savior. Tell Him your fears and your pains. Pour out all your questions and all your emotions on Jesus. Ask for His help and His comfort because He doesn't want you to be alone. While others around you may not understand or may not be able to help, Jesus does understand and He will be at your side. We can bring our own sufferings or the sufferings of our friends, our family and our community to Jesus. We do not have to suffer alone. We have a choice. We can go it alone or we can come to Jesus. Feel the comfort as He reaches down from heaven to you. Let Him help you with His wisdom and power for your life.

- What is your greatest affliction or agony right now? Write it down in one or two sentences and then spend time in prayer telling Jesus about it and asking for His guidance and help.

27 Torn Curtain-Matthew 27:45-54

Context: Matthew writes his gospel to the Jews. He includes the detail of the tearing of the curtain in the temple. Jews would understand that this curtain had separated a holy God from a sinful people. With sin paid for on the cross, God was no longer separated from His forgiven people.

The curtain was 30 feet high by 30 feet wide. It separated the Holy Place in the temple from the Holy of Holies. It separated sinful men from the earthly dwelling of the holy and perfect God. No one could enter behind the curtain except the high priest on the Day of Atonement. If he or anyone else entered at any other time they died. Man was separated from God by sin. Oddly, today man separates himself from God to embrace sin. The numbers of Christians practicing their faith or reading the Bible continues to dwindle. Fewer and fewer know the simple stories of the Bible or have the knowledge of who God is. Our society has proclaimed God is dead. We separate ourselves because we are afraid of God and realize that our sin makes it impossible to come near God by ourselves.

Good Friday brought an end to the separation symbolized by the curtain. The cost was borne by Jesus on the cross. He took our sins upon Himself and that sin separated Him from God. "About the ninth hour Jesus cried out in a loud voice, "Eloi, Eloi, lama sabachthani?"--which means, "My God, my God, why have you forsaken me?" (v.46) Bearing our sins, Jesus stood on the outside of the curtain and was separated from the Father. He longed for the comfort that He had always had from the Father, but our sin denied him. He carried the sins of the world forcing God to turn His back on His Son. Jesus goes through the agony of Hell, the separation that comes because of sin, in order to pay the penalty of sin. Why did God forsake Him? God turned His back on Jesus that day so that He would not have to forsake us.

On the Day of Atonement, a lamb was sacrificed, and the High Priest was allowed to take the blood of that lamb through the curtain and into the Holy of Holies as an offering for the sins of man. On Good Friday, Jesus as our High Priest sacrificed Himself and took His blood as an offering for our sins. It happened at the moment of His death. "And when Jesus had cried out again in a loud voice, he gave up his spirit." (v.50) It was the perfect payment for the sins of every man and woman who ever lived. The imperfect sacrifices of animals were no longer necessary. They had shown the severity of sin. Jesus' sacrifice was the payment for sin. With that payment, the separation between God and man was over.

With the separation over, the curtain in the temple was removed by God. At the moment of Jesus' death, the temple curtain tore in two. "At that moment the curtain of the temple was torn in two from top to bottom. The earth shook and the rocks split." (v.51) Anyone working in the Holy Place that day must have been horrified. Up till then, anyone who entered or looked into the Most Holy Place would have died. Yet, no priest died that day. Man was no longer separated from God. Man could come into the very presence of God and embrace a God who loved them so much that He sacrificed His son for them. Man could now have the love that was denied Jesus on the cross.

The Old Testament saints were always kept separate from God. They could not come near Mount Sinai when the law was given. They could not enter the Most Holy Place because of their sin. Yet our churches have no places that are forbidden to us. The sacrifice of Jesus has torn the curtain that separates us from God and has given us free access to the Father. We come before Him as a church to pray at His altar and to receive Holy Communion. We come before Him in our prayers and every time we open up the pages of scripture. We have a full access pass to God that allows us to cast our cares on Him in prayer and receive blessings from this loving God as we share an intimate fellowship with Him.

I wonder if Old Testament saints felt distant from God. They could come to the temple, but a layman was always outside the temple building. The building and the curtain separated them from a God who punished any who came too close. Today, the curtain is torn. You can come and pray at the altar of your church. You can look upon a picture of Jesus and see God in the flesh and speak to the one who understands what it is like to be human and need to eat and sleep. You have the opportunity to come behind the curtain and spend time with your God in ways that few Old Testament people ever did.

There is no reason to be separate from God. Jesus has brought down the curtain.

- With the curtain down, what would you like to say to Jesus? What keep you from daily time with Jesus in prayer?

28 Honoring Jesus-John 19:31-42

Context: One would have expected Jesus' disciples or mother

to claim the body, but neither could have gained an audience

with Pilate to ask for the body. Instead, two men risked their

futures to lovingly honor Jesus in death.

My father and mother in law are buried in the military cemetery

at Rock Island, Illinois. It is a beautiful place where the stones

are laid out in perfect rows and the lawn is meticulously kept.

The 21-gun salute and the presentation of the flag to the

family of the serviceman or woman are our nation's way of

honoring those who served in the armed forces. Families

come to the service to honor their loved ones as well. They

place flowers at the graves. They tell stories to remind

themselves of what this person meant to them and to others.

The honor follows death. Such is the story of Jesus' burial and

the men who honored Him by lovingly laying Him to rest.

The Jewish Sanhedrin hated Jesus and had brought Jesus to

be crucified. Two of their members, Joseph and Nicodemus,

secretly believed in Jesus but did so cautiously. The horrific death of Jesus caused them to throw caution aside. "Later, Joseph of Arimathea asked Pilate for the body of Jesus. Now Joseph was a disciple of Jesus, but secretly because he feared the Jews." (v.38) Touched by Jesus during their lives, they could not abandon Him in death. Being part of the upper circle of Jewish society, they alone could ask for an audience with Pilate to save the body of Jesus from a criminal's grave. Their actions may have meant expulsion from the Sanhedrin because this group hated Jesus so much, but the pair wanted to show honor to the one they loved.

After thirty-nine lashes and six hours on the cross, Jesus body must have been in horrid shape. The two men give dignity to the battered body of our Lord. "Taking Jesus' body, the two of them wrapped it, with the spices, in strips of linen. This was in accordance with Jewish burial customs." (v.40) With tenderness and sorrow, they wrap the body of Jesus with linens and seventy-five pounds of spices. The body that was beaten and humiliated in His final hours of life was given a proper Jewish burial with respect and dignity. The two men must have planned the burial during the hours while Jesus was on the cross. They gathered all the resources that were needed to prepare Jesus at the moment that Pilate released the body to them. Jesus died in humiliation but would be buried with honor.

A new tomb was nearby. It was Joseph's tomb (Matt. 27:60) and it was used for the burial of Jesus. "At the place where Jesus was crucified, there was a garden, and in the garden a new tomb, in which no one had ever been laid." (v.41) No expense would be spared to honor Jesus. Nicodemus had brought expensive spices. Joseph would give Jesus a place to lie with the rich in death (Isaiah 53:9). No word was said about the cost. It was the least that they could do for this one who had done so much for others. The time was short. The Passover was quickly coming. Yet, the men were determined to honor Jesus with their possessions and give the slain Jesus the dignity that He deserved in death.

It was an act of love as they honored the Savior. They repaid the kindness that He had shown many people. They did what they could to undo the dishonor that the Sanhedrin had shown Him. You and I have the ability to honor a risen Lord. We can honor Jesus for all the things that He has done for us in our life. He healed you when you were sick. He died so that we might have forgiveness. Yet, unlike the two men at the tomb, we also can honor Jesus for all the things that we know He will continue to do for us. We know that Jesus is alive. We know that He will take us to be with Him in heaven. We know that Jesus will answer our prayers and comfort our hurts. He is worthy of honor for all he does in our past, our present and our future.

We have the opportunity to honor a living Jesus with our lives. We can boldly identify with our Jesus not worried about what people will say if they find we have faith. We can speak tenderly and with respect to Jesus in our prayers realizing that we have a gracious friend. We can make sacrifices to honor Him by caring for others or using our resources for His ministry. We can honor Him because of what He has and continues to do in our lives. We can honor Him so that others may know what He has done for us and for them. Our Lord had honored us by all the things that He has done. Like Joseph and Nicodemus, we have the opportunity to honor Him and show Him and others how special Jesus is and always will be to us.

- How can you honor Jesus? Is there someone who needs His care or someone who needs to know of His love that you can serve to honor your Lord?

29 Darkness Turns to Joy-Matt. 28:1-10

Context: It was early on the Sunday morning that we now call Easter. Jesus' body had been hurriedly prepared on Friday before the Passover began. The women who came to finish the burial preparations had a surprise as their sorrow turn to joy.

The Saturday before Easter must have been the darkest day that the disciples ever experienced. For three years they had experienced the joy of following Jesus around the Holy Land. The miracles and messages that they had seen with Jesus must have been amazing. Now He was gone. He was taken from them in an instant when they were not ready and not prepared. At times, sadness abounds in our world as well. We lose our job, or our parent gets sick. We have a child that is struggling, or we just wonder how to pay the bills. Life gets tough and we wonder where to turn. The answer is, of course, to come to Jesus, but what does that mean? The answer is found in Easter and if we are not careful, we will miss it. The answer lies in three words: listen, obey and trust.

Those who listen to Jesus have hope. The angel is there to remind the women what Jesus has already told them. "He is not here; he has risen, just as he said. Come and see the place where he lay." (v.6) Jesus told His disciples on several occasions that He was going to rise from the dead. If they had listened to Him, Saturday could have been different. They could have spent all of Saturday just waiting for Jesus to come to life. The day would have been one of expectation, not sorrow. The worry and doubt could have been replaced with hope and anticipation. Hope begins by knowing what God has promised and holding onto those promises. If we listen, God will always prepare us for what is to come. He will always help us be ready to make the most of the joy.

Having heard the message, the women were told to obey a task that God gave them. They were to go and tell the disciples. "Then go quickly and tell his disciples: 'He has risen from the dead and is going ahead of you into Galilee. There you will see him.' Now I have told you." (v.7) When you have heard what Jesus says, you are to obey. It is only if the disciples go to Galilee that they will have the full future that the

Lord has in mind for them. They will see Jesus later that day

on Easter, but it will be in Galilee that the disciples will get the

full instructions and understanding of what the resurrection

means. Just standing in Jerusalem will not overcome their

fears. Jesus wants them to participate in their future. Come to

Galilee He says so that I can prepare you for what is to come.

The final step was one of trust. They were afraid. "So, the

women hurried away from the tomb, afraid yet filled with joy,

and ran to tell his disciples." They had expected to embalm

the body of Jesus and had just heard the news that Jesus was

alive. They needed to believe the message and trust the

angel. Jesus had prepared them for the resurrection. An angel

had told them it was true. Yet, they trembled as they let it all

soak in. Slowly their doubts melted away and they believed

what they had been told. It is faith that makes hope a reality.

You have to believe what Jesus has said and trust Him with

your life. Trust will overcome the doubts and bring joy for

Jesus always keeps His promises.

God works in ways and at times we don't expect. Imagine the

women's surprise when they arrived at the tomb and found the stone rolled away. As they looked in, they saw that God's plan of salvation was complete. They had been sorrowful and had not even thought about asking God for help. God will surprise you, too. In our dark days, He is working on behalf of his people even when they don't see Him working. He will heal their illnesses, help them find jobs and raise their kids. We may feel lucky when things work out, but luck doesn't bring us hope. Luck is fickle and can be good or bad. Only when we start depending on God to help can we get past the dark days. Only when we start expecting Him to be at the tomb or any other place where we have problems and questions will we have true hope and joy.

The stone was rolled back so that people could see for themselves what God had done for them. Sometimes, God rolls away the things that keep us from seeing His hand in our lives. He helps us see with eyes of faith what others miss. The change in the disciples when they saw the resurrection was amazing. The same disciples who had not believed the women (Luke 24:11) were declaring the resurrection to thousands on Pentecost. As Christians experience the power of the resurrection in their lives, it changes them. The sadness disappears and we start to rely on the Lord to help us in every aspect of life. When days are dark, we need to look to Jesus for a glorious Sunday. May we trust Him to help when we can see His work and when He works behind the scenes in our lives.

- What is the darkest day that you have had recently? How does it help that Jesus is ready and able to help bring light and joy to your sorrow?

30 Seeing Is Believing? - John 20:01-9

Context: Early on Easter morning, Mary Magdalene had gone to the tomb and found Jesus missing. She runs to the disciples who send Peter and John to investigate. Both see the empty grave, but only one believes. The three words used to talk about seeing show what it takes to believe when you see.

It is easy for a Christian to wonder why his or her non-Christian friends just can't see the truth about Jesus. The Easter story is all around them, but they still don't understand, and they refuse to believe. The truth is that seeing doesn't always produce belief. Think of a magician sawing a woman in half. You see the trick, but your mind refuses to believe what your eyes say is happening. For some, the resurrection of Jesus seems impossible as well. Most people have heard the story, but they refuse to believe it because it just doesn't make sense. Sometimes that is because they have just glanced at the cross. Other times they may have seriously thought about it and struggled to believe what seems impossible to them. In John's account of the resurrection, we find three instances of seeing, but only one believes as well.

Both Peter and John ran to the tomb when they heard Mary Magdalene's report, but John was younger and he got there first. The original Greek word says that he "glanced" in the tomb. "He (John) bent over and looked in at the strips of linen lying there but did not go in." (v.5) He may have been out of breath and took a quick glance while Peter caught up to him. He probably only had a few moments to look before Peter was there. The proof of Jesus' resurrection was in plain sight, but the meaning didn't fully register with his mind. His look was quick and affirmed what Mary had said. Jesus was not there. The tomb was empty. His eyes saw the grave clothes, but the glance was succinct, and his mind didn't have time to process what he saw.

Bold Peter arrives shortly after John and goes in to see what has happened for himself. The Greek word says that he "considered carefully" what he saw. "Then Simon Peter, who was behind him, arrived and went into the tomb. He saw the strips of linen lying there," (v.6) Perhaps Peter not only looked but also gazed intently at the strips of cloth. He stood for a moment and noticed that the head's burial cloth was folded up carefully and laid by itself. Peter would have considered all the facts, but he couldn't make any sense out of what he saw. Like a person watching a magician, he could not believe his eyes. Jesus should be lying before him. The truth was obvious, but Peter dismissed the truth because it could not be. He saw the facts but didn't know what to make of them. When John finally enters the tomb, he also sees the linens and the burial cloth. The Greek word says that he "perceived" what had happened. "Finally the other disciple (John), who had reached the tomb first, also went inside. He saw and believed." (v.8) John believed in the resurrection because he didn't let the impossible stop him from understanding what must have happened. The text tells us that he didn't understand fully what it meant, but he knew what had happened. The grave clothes were lying there as if the body of Jesus had just passed right through them. He saw the truth and accepted it as fact because there was nothing else that made sense. The same Jesus who had raised Lazarus and Jairus' daughter from the dead was now alive.

Many people around us have merely glanced at the resurrection of Jesus. They see the empty cross on a church yard. They have a relative who is going to church on Easter. They take a fleeting look at Jesus before they go back to life. They never stop to consider what the empty cross or Easter celebration is all about. Others have heard the story or read about the resurrection in a book, but it just seems too impossible to believe. People do not rise from the dead. The disciples must have stolen the body or fabricated the Easter resurrection story. Some will not believe the story because they can't believe what they have seen and heard. It doesn't make sense and so it must not be true.

John had the perfect opportunity to tell Peter what he saw and believed on the way back from the tomb. Did John tell Peter about his suspicions or did he silently ponder them for himself? The key to helping others believe is for us to keep telling the story. Those who have only glanced at Easter may be confronted with new details for the first time. Those who have heard the story and rejected it need to hear the story again from a fresh perspective. They need to hear why you believe the impossible is true. They need to hear how the empty tomb is your hope for eternal life and how this living Jesus is active in your life. As you walk away from the empty tomb, tell others what you believe so that they can "see" the risen Jesus for themselves and believe.

- Why do you believe that Jesus has risen? Who do you know who needs to hear how this living Jesus is active in your life?

31 Wait patiently For Jesus - John 20:11-18

Context: It is still Easter morning. The first women have come and gone and so have the two disciples. Mary Magdalene lingers at the tomb confused and crying. Her patience and love would be rewarded as she saw and touched Jesus.

Patience is truly a virtue. We gave up and left the restaurant minutes before our friend finally came. We hung up after a long time only to find later that the doctor was just about to answer our call. We want things now and we find it hard to wait. Yet those who wait patiently are often rewarded especially if they are waiting for Jesus. We know He is listening to our prayers. We know that He is working on our problems. Our problem is that we often want the solution before it is ready. Those who wait patiently for the Lord will find that he will dry their tears and take away their doubts. Other people may not always be worth the wait, but Jesus will always help us with what we need.

John and Peter came to the tomb, saw that it was empty and left. Mary Magdalene stayed. She was looking for her Jesus.

The angels sitting in the tomb asked her why she is crying.

Jesus will ask her about her tears as well. She is so upset that

she doesn't notice that the answer to her prayers is standing

at her side. "At this, she turned around and saw Jesus

standing there, but she did not realize that it was Jesus."

(v.14) Perhaps, she was kept from knowing Him like the two

men on the road to Emmaus (Luke 24:15). Perhaps her grief

kept her from seeing or expecting Jesus at her side. She

wanted answers but feared the worst. She had to know where

the one she loved had been taken.

All Jesus had to do was speak her name and Mary recognized

her Lord and friend. "Jesus said to her, "Mary." She turned

toward him and cried out in Aramaic, "Rabboni!" (which means

Teacher)." (v.16) Having turned away from the man she

thought was the gardener, she turned toward Jesus to see His

face. Her heart had been filled with blinding grief, but she

recognized her teacher's voice. He had not forgotten her but

had returned to the tomb just so that He could bring comfort

and joy to this one that He loved. Her suffering had been

replaced by delight. Jesus was alive. Her patience had been

rewarded. She was the first to see the risen Lord and to know the certainty of the resurrection.

She grabbed hold of Jesus and held Him close. Now that she had found Jesus once again, she did not want to let Him go. Yet, Jesus reassured her that there was no reason to fear. She could let Him go for she would see Him again. "Jesus said, "Do not hold on to me, for I have not yet returned to the Father." (v.17) The time of the ascension was days away. She did not have to panic for this was not their final meeting. She needed to let Jesus go so that He could appear to others like the men on the way to Emmaus (Luke 24:13f) and perhaps to Peter (1 Cor. 15:5). She needed to let Him go because Jesus had a task for her to do. She needed to let others know that He was alive.

She had patiently waited for answers. Now she was to go and tell the disciples whom Jesus loved about His resurrection. "Go instead to my brothers and tell them, 'I am returning to my Father and your Father, to my God and your God." (v.17b) They would be as upset as Mary had been about Jesus' death. It was time for them to hear the news so that when He did appear to them as well, they would be ready to believe. There are others around us crying because they think that Jesus has not heard their prayers or because they think Jesus doesn't care. When we see Jesus' answer for us, we need to share that answer so that others can be ready for His answer to their prayers. Our joy and confidence in Jesus can be infectious. When the Lord helps us, it can encourage those who are still waiting for His answers and help.

Patience with Jesus is often rewarded. We can depend on our Lord to hear our cries and to come and help us at just the right time. Every trial and problem give us a chance to see Jesus in a new way. As we experience our troubles and His aid, we see the depth of His care for us. When we feel like giving up, we need to keep praying because we know He hears us. When we feel empty, we need to keep reading His word for His answers are found in its pages. Each trial is a chance to hear the Lord speak our name and show His love so that we can share that love with others who are struggling to be patient in their need.

- What is one answer to prayer that you are still

waiting for? Why can you be confident that Jesus will

answer your prayer?

32 Disappointed With Easter? - Luke 24:13-32

Context: It is late afternoon into the evening on Easter. The news that some have seen Jesus alive has been circulating through Jerusalem, but the significance of His resurrection is still beyond their understanding. A special visit from Jesus changes all that and shows us why Easter is so important.

Are you disappointed with Easter? As American holidays go, it isn't much of a holiday anymore. People don't usually get any extra time off. There are no presents or fireworks. It isn't even the beginning of summer like Memorial Day. What is the most important day of the church year is hardly important to many people in our world. It reminds us the two men on the road to Emmaus. They have heard the story of the empty tomb just like many people in our world and are disappointed. Jesus had done some great miracles and taught amazing things, but now He is gone. Instead of celebrating the empty tomb, they were going home because it was all over. What a disappointment. As the story unfolds, we see three reasons for their disappointment.

The first thing that you notice is that their Jesus was too small. They understood Jesus as just a great prophet but not a Messiah. "What things?" he asked. "About Jesus of Nazareth," they replied. "He was a prophet, powerful in word and deed before God and all the people." (v.19) Jesus had done some impressive miracles, but now He was martyred and it was all over. They had assumed that He was special, but it turned out that He was just another in a long line of prophets from the Lord. He lived, He told His message and the Jews killed Him just like they had killed so many of the other prophets. They never saw Jesus as anything but a great teacher. Now they would have to wait for the next prophet. Maybe he would be the Messiah that would change everything.

In their mind, Jesus had failed because they had the wrong expectations of what the Messiah was supposed to do. "we had hoped that he was the one who was going to redeem Israel." (v.21) They wanted a Palm Sunday Messiah and not a Good Friday/Easter Savior. They saw the Messiah coming into town and defeating the Romans. They saw the Messiah bringing glory and comfort to the people of Israel so that they would be the envy of the world. They ignored the Old Testament passages about a suffering servant and a Messiah who would save the people from their sin. As Jesus came in on Palm Sunday, He seemed like their Messiah. When He died on the cross, He seemed like a failure because they didn't think that they needed a savior from sin.

Their expectations about Jesus made them miss the obvious truth. The men were going home on early Easter evening. They had heard the truth but could not believe it. "They went to the tomb early this morning but didn't find his body. They came and told us that they had seen a vision of angels, who said he was alive." (v.22-23) The women reported what the angel said. Mary Magdalene told them what Jesus had said. None of it made sense and none of it seemed believable.

You wonder what the men needed. Did they need the angel choir of Christmas? Did they need God speaking from the heavens? The proof was all around them and instead of celebrating, they were going home with heavy hearts.

Easter is often disappointing for the same reasons today. Many have a Jesus that is too small. Our world often sees

Jesus as just a great teacher with a moral code or helpful hints that might make life better. We often try and fashion Jesus to meet our needs. We want a Jesus that accepts us as we are. We want a Jesus who is part Father Christmas and part Tooth Fairy giving us everything we want with no strings attached. Because Jesus doesn't match our picture of what our God should be; many people miss the truth about Jesus and about Easter. They know about the cross and the empty tomb. They have the witness of millions of Christians who would rather die than abandon Jesus. All of that means nothing and so Easter means nothing.

The cure is simple. We need to humble ourselves and see the passion of Jesus. The disciples from Emmaus started getting excited when Jesus began to explain the scripture to them. "And beginning with Moses and all the Prophets, he explained to them what was said in all the Scriptures concerning himself." (v.27) As we learn about Jesus and His passion, we will begin to see that the real Jesus is greater than all the false versions that the world has created of Him. The real Jesus is amazing and worth knowing. As we listen to Him in His word, we build a relationship with Jesus and catch His passion for the salvation of all. We rush to tell others as these men did so that they can have salvation, too. Jesus passion becomes our passion. We see what Jesus did for us and how much He loves us. Our hearts are on fire. We see the importance of Easter and have a passion for sharing Jesus with the world.

- Why is Easter so central to the passion of Jesus? Why should this passion be so important to you and me?

Bible Studies

All pages of this student guide may be copied for a local church or small group use. - taken from "32 days with Christ's Passion" by Mark R. Etter ©2016

02 Love Stands Out-Mark 14:1-9

Angus McMahon stood tall with his wife at his side and his hands on the shoulders of two little girls. The mayor was reading a proclamation making this Angus McMahon day for this brave firefighter's rescue of the two girls who stood in front of him. When the girls beamed at him in the middle of the ceremony, Angus almost lost it. He felt their love and knew that he now had a connection to these two girls for the rest of their lives.

In the days before Palm Sunday, one woman shared her love with Jesus. John's gospel tells us that it was Mary, the sister of Lazarus who Jesus had raised from the dead. Pouring her perfume on Jesus' head filled the room with the scent of love. Her selfless act is criticized, but Jesus accepts her gift and defends her before the disciples. One wonders how much this act of love must have meant to Jesus as He entered the dark days to come. Mary teaches us to keep showing God's love even if others don't understand our gift.

1. If you had fifty thousand dollars to spend on someone in your family, what would you buy?

2. When and where did the events of this story take place? (14:1-3)

3. What amazing thing did a woman do while Jesus was visiting Bethany? (14:3) Why would this woman make this great a sacrifice for Jesus? (Hint: see John 11)

4. What reaction did the woman's actions get? What was suggested as a better use for this gift? (14:4-5)

5. What extravagant thing would you like to do for Jesus if you had the money even if others might think is a waste?

6. **Whom did Jesus rebuke? How did Jesus justify Mary's actions?** (14:6-8)

7. **What did Jesus predict?** (14:9) **How did that make this a special opportunity to worship Jesus?**

8. **What do you think Jesus meant when He said: "She did what she could"?** (14:8)

9. **What can we learn about values from the woman in this story?** (14:9)

10. **Mary was criticized for her act of selfless sacrifice. What keeps you from showing your love for Jesus and from making sacrifices for Him?**

03 What Did You Expect? - Luke 19:28-44

John had been the salesman of the year and so the company promoted him. Looking back, it seemed like the worst thing that they could have done to him. There were more pay and prestige, but now he was administering others and not doing the sales calls that he really loved and was successful at. The company had expectations of him that he struggled to reach. He had no experience running an office or managing others. He finally went to his boss and asked for his old job back. He just wanted to be the person God had made him.

Jesus comes riding into Jerusalem and the Passover amid the cheering of the crowds. Here was their Messiah and king. Surely, He would take up residence in Jerusalem and bring back Israel's glory. Sadly, the crowd didn't know Jesus. He was not the earthly king that they were looking for, but rather the savior that they needed. In the days ahead, Jesus would fulfill the ministry that the Father had given Him. Many would leave Jesus, but those who let Him be the Savior and Lord found a friend who would change their lives.

1. What is your favorite part of a parade? Why do you think people like parades so much?

2. Jesus starts out in Bethany. How close is this to Jerusalem? (19:29) What other events happened in Bethany?

3. What instructions does Jesus give to two of the disciples? (19:30-31) What challenge does Jesus foresee?

4. When has Jesus given you a task that seemed impossible? How did Jesus prepare you for the challenge?

5. How do you picture the scene in verses 35-38? If you had been there, what sounds would you have

heard and what emotions would have been present in the people around you?

6. What kind of reception do you think Jesus would get if He came to your town today?

7. What do the people call Jesus as He entered the city? (19:38) What hopes or dreams of the people do those titles convey?

8. What has God done for you recently that made you want to shout it out or tell others?

9. What do the Pharisees want Jesus to tell the crowd? (19:39) Why do you think that the Pharisees in the crowd are upset?

10. What expectations do you have of Jesus? What do you want Him to come and bring into your life?

06 The Joy of Serving-John 13 1-17

Pastor Bob looked around as he pulled up at the church on Sunday morning and noticed that the parking lot was full of snow. He went looking for the rusty orange shovel and finding it, began to shovel the sidewalks and the handicapped parking spots. One by one, the members of the church came. Tom had a shovel in his trunk and he began to help. Nancy swept the snow off the sidewalks near the building. Bill found some rock salt and began to spread it on the sidewalks so that they didn't refreeze. Soon, much of the parking lot was clear and the rest was passable. It was amazing how one person's example led them all to care for each other.

Jesus knew that Peter would deny Him and Judas would betray Him. He also knew that the disciples would all desert Him on His arrest. Yet, He wanted to show them the extent of His love and teach them a valuable lesson about service. He and the disciples were gathered in the upper room to celebrate the Passover Festival. As the meal began, no one had taken the time to wash the dirty feet of those who had come for the meal. Jesus showed that all of us are called to serve by taking a towel in order to wash and dry each of the disciple's feet. The lesson is simple. If He, the Son of God, is willing to serve such a lowly task, then there is no task that should be below any of us.

1. **How beautiful are your feet? (Model ready, never looked, or feet like a troll)**

2. **What does Jesus know that the disciples have not figured out? (13:1)**

3. **Describe the scene in verses 3-5. What do you think motivated Jesus to wash their feet?**

4. **Describe a person you know who has demonstrated unselfish service to others? What do you think makes them special?**

5. How does Peter react to Jesus' service? (13:6-8) How does Jesus respond to Peter's refusal to be served?

6. How do you react when a superior unexpectedly serves you?

7. What does Jesus mean when He says, "Unless I wash you; you will have no part of me?" (13:8)

8. In what way does Jesus wash our feet today? What are the consequences of refusing Jesus' love and service?

9. How does Jesus challenge our ideas of leadership? (13:14-16) Why do we honor those who serve?

10. In what areas do you struggle to be humble? Who would benefit from your humble service today?

09 The way to God-John 14:1-14

Whir. Whir. Whir. Each time that Larry tried to get out of the snowdrift, the tires spun even faster. He looked at Sandy and the kids and announced that he would walk back about a half mile to the convenience store to get help. Sandy looked at him, but before she could say a word, he said, "There is still plenty of light and it isn't that far. I'll be back for all of you very soon." With that, he began to walk away. True to his word, he was back in a half hour riding in a pickup truck. "This nice gentleman has a chain and will have us out in no time".

The section opens and ends with our Lord's comforting words, "Let not your heart be troubled." It should be no surprise that the disciples were struggling. Jesus had predicted Judas' betrayal (John 13:21) and Peter's denial (John 13:38). Yet the hardest words for the disciples to deal with were the words that Jesus was going to leave them (John 13:33). Questions circled their minds and fears began to take hold of them. Jesus would comfort them and

let them know why He must go. Jesus assures all of us
that heaven is a real place prepared for us and that He will
come back and bring us there at the proper time.

1. **What is your greatest fear about the future?**

2. **What comfort does Jesus give His disciples? (14:2-3)**

3. **How does Jesus have your future covered? How is Jesus helping you with your life today?**

4. **What is Thomas' question to Jesus? (14:5) Put Jesus' answer in your own words? (14:6-7)**

5. **How is Jesus the way and truth in your life? (14:6)**

6. **What question does Jesus ask the disciples? (14:9)**

7. What tone of voice do you imagine Jesus speaking to His disciples? How does Jesus speak to you when you want your own way?

8. How would you respond to someone who says there are many ways to God?

9. What promise does Jesus make to those who have faith in Him? (14:12-13)

10. What greater things do you want to ask God to let you do with your life? How would those ministries impact others?

13 Be Transformed With Joy-John 16:16-33

Jamie was sick and tired of being pregnant. She waddled into every room and found it hard to find anything that fit. She just felt tired of feeling fat. Surely, having the baby would be easier. Then the night of the delivery came. As she sweated and strained with every push, she hated her husband and wished she had never gotten pregnant. Suddenly, delivery was over and the nurse put her little girl into her arms. Jamie immediately forgot about all the pain and looked into the blue eyes straining to stare at her. She looked forward to a lifetime of getting to know and love this child that God had brought into her life.

As Jesus concluded His teaching with the disciples on Thursday night, He dealt with their emotions. They were sad, confused and afraid because of what He had said to them. He brought them a message of joy. While they were definitely not feeling joyful that night, He promised that the events that lie ahead would turn their sorrow to joy. It would be a joy that would come from inside as the Holy

Spirit helped them understand and gave them faith. The disciples were real men and faced the same kind of struggles that we often have. Their struggles remind us that we can have that same kind of joy, too.

1. **What was your most difficult or confusing class in school? What emotions rise up in you as you think of that class?**

2. **What is Jesus referring to in verse 16? What tone do you hear in the disciples' voices in verses 17-18?**

3. **How do you deal with confusing passages in scripture?**

4. **What is Jesus' explanation in verse 20? Looking at Good Friday and Easter, how did His words come true?**

5. What analogy did Jesus use to further explain His departure? (16:21) In what ways does the woman feel pain and joy in childbirth?

6. When have you felt pain as you served others? How did God bring joy in that situation?

7. What power have the disciples not unlocked? (16:23-24) What promises are made about the power of prayer in these verses?

8. How is the relationship to the Father described? (16:27) How is our relationship with God the key to joy?

9. How well do you deal with change? How have the challenges and pains of life helped you grow?

10. What is the difference between the joy promised by the world and the joy promised by Jesus?

16 Broken Sanctuary-Luke 22:39-48

It had been a brutal three weeks. The Parkinson deal had drained everything out of Tom. He had come to Estes Park for a few days off. He drove up to Bear Lake so he could hike the trail to Emerald Lake. He let the trail push the last couple days away and reconnect him with memories of hiking this trail with his dad. Sitting on the edge of Emerald Lake, he glanced at Hallett Peak and began to pray about God's greatness. Shortly before sunset, he slowly walked down to Bear Lake. As he drove back to the hotel, his cell phone started chirping. He knew that something had gone wrong back at work. His quiet vacation had been interrupted.

Having spent the evening with the disciples at the last supper, Jesus wanted sanctuary before He faced the cross. He came to Gethsemane and began to pray. Here was a place where He could find quiet and time to be with the Father. Wrapped in the arms of the Father, He drew comfort and courage for what lay ahead. As we face struggles, it is nice to know that we have the sanctuary of prayer as well.

1. Where do you go when you want to be alone and think? What makes that place special?

2. What does this passage reveal about Jesus's habits? (Luke 22:39) Why is time at Gethsemane important to Jesus as He prepares for the cross?

3. What does Jesus ask the disciples to pray for? (Luke 22:40) Why was such a prayer so important?

4. Jesus prays "yours (will) be done" in verse 42. What does Jesus' prayer reveal about His own character and His relationship with the Father?

5. When you find yourself in a difficult situation, do you pray for deliverance or for strength to do what

is right? What is the difference and what did Jesus pray for?

6. What does this passage tell us about Jesus' physical and emotional condition shortly before His death? (22:44) How was Jesus strengthened at this difficult time? (22:43)

7. What would times of regular prayer bring to your life when you face painful or difficult times?

8. What did Jesus find the disciples doing when He returned to them? (22:45) What was the reason for their exhaustion?

9. How do Jesus' actions and attitudes compare to the disciples in this time of crisis? Which are more effective and why?

10. What does Jesus teach us in Gethsemane about the sanctuary of prayer? What is one area in your life where prayer could bring greater peace?

18 Don't give in to evil-Mark 14:53-65

Frank was having a great night with his friends. The group had gone to the movies and now were just hanging out at the mall. They went into the dime store and Tim challenged them all to try to shoplift a small item for fun. Frank was horrified and told them that he wouldn't do it. Not only that, he would rat them out as they left the store. His buddies grumbled and shot angry glances at him as they left the store empty handed. The man at the cash register stopped the group and thanked Frank and then pointed to the cameras on the ceiling. "You just saved your buddies some jail time."

Having been arrested, Jesus was brought to the house of Caiaphas so that the chief priests could find evidence and make their case against Jesus. The "trial" was filled with false evidence that didn't match. Finally, the high priest asks Jesus to incriminate himself in violation of Jewish law. Jesus is a model for all of what to do when evil attacks. He is quiet when the room is filled with lies but is not afraid to answer to the truth. Don't give in to evil, but keep your character so that the Lord can protect you.

1. What injustice do you see in our society?

2. Who was gathered together (14:53) and what was their purpose? (14:55)

3. What perversions of justice do you see in this "trial"? (14:55-61)

4. Why do you think Jesus remained silent as these accusations were made? (14:61)

5. How do you act when someone accuses you? Why do you feel compelled to react this way?

6. What does the high priest ask in order to force Jesus to speak? (14:61) How does Jesus answer? (14:62)

7. Jesus went on to say "And you will see the Son of Man sitting at the right hand of the Mighty One and coming on the clouds of heaven." (14:62) What is Jesus predicting will happen on the last day? How will the High Priest feel then?

8. Why did the High Priest tear his clothes? (14:63) What did they feel was blasphemous about Jesus's statement?

9. What punishment did the chief priest pronounce on Jesus? (14:64) How did the Jews show their disdain for Jesus? (14:65)

10. How does Jesus' behavior differ from the behavior of the chief priests and elders? What can you learn

from Jesus about dealing with those who oppose

you?

21 Looking for loopholes-Luke 23:1-25

My twenty-something adult children for years insisted that my wife and I have an Easter egg hunt for them as we did when they were children. It had been our custom to hide a few eggs with money in it. I thought that this should be the last year for Easter egg hunts and so I put an IOU in one of the eggs. "This certificate good for five dollars except in the states of Kentucky, Ohio, Indiana, and Illinois". I thought I had the kids because those were all the states we regularly visited. Three years later, I was proven wrong. We were visiting West Virginia and my son pulled the certificate out of his wallet and requested his five dollars. I guess not every loophole can stand the test of time.

We know Pilate's name from the Apostle's Creed. He was the governor of Judea for about ten years. His word was law and the Romans were in full control of Palestine. Yet, he will be remembered as the man who tried Jesus and knew that Jesus was innocent but sent Him off to the cross anyway. He is afraid of the Jews and tries to do the right thing in the wrong way. Instead of just proclaiming Jesus to be innocent, Pilate tries to find a loophole that will get both Jesus and Pilate off the hook. It doesn't work.

1. What do you think it would be like to be on trial? How would it affect your life and your family?

2. What is the charge against Jesus before Pilate? (23:2) How is this charge different than the charge that the Sanhedrin made? (see Mark 14:64)

3. What is Pilate's first question to Jesus? (23:3) Why do you think Pilate determined Jesus was innocent even though Jesus admits that He is a king?

4. Sometimes Jesus is silent before His accusers, sometimes He speaks. What do you learn from Jesus about how to respond to your accusers?

5. The Jews feel Jesus slipping away from their hands. What charge do they make to persuade Pilate? (23:5)

6. Why was Herod anxious to see Jesus? (23:8) How serious a threat does Herod think Jesus really is?

7. Having failed to wash his hands of Jesus by sending Him to Herod, how does Pilate try to reason with the Jews (23:15-16)

8. Why is it difficult to reason with unjust people?

9. What is Pilate's desire for Jesus? (23:22) In what way did the crowds influence Pilate's actions?

10. When do you find it hardest to stand up to the crowd? What would you have done in Pilate's place?

24 Forsaken-Matt. 27:32-50

Tammy went to a party at a friend's house and ended up pregnant with a boy that she barely knew. As the pregnancy started showing, people began to treat her differently. Many of her friends kept their distance. A young man that she liked would have nothing to do with her. Even her parents refused to talk about how she was going to finish High School with a newborn. Finally, an older woman named Thelma at her church took Tammy under her wing. She helped Tammy create her own plan for finishing High School and even for going on to get her associate's degree. She talked with Tammy's mom about the plans and even volunteered to watch the baby twice a week. She was the one true friend that Tammy had during this dark time in her life.

In His last hours, Jesus received very little comfort or support. Having faced six trials through the night and early morning and been beaten by Jew and Roman alike, Jesus is expected to carry his cross. He cannot do it and a stranger is enlisted for the task. The Romans took His clothes and the

Jews stood before the cross and made fun of Him. Only one of His disciples dared to come to the cross (John 19:25-27) and the women watched from a distance (verses 55-56). When we feel lonely or lost, we know that we can turn to Jesus.

1. Describe a time you felt all alone? What would it have meant to have a friend by your side?

2. Who is forced to carry Jesus' cross? (27:32) Why does Jesus need this help?

3. Having nailed Jesus to a cross, what do the soldiers do with his possessions? (27:35-36)

4. What do you think it was like being hung naked in a public place for hours?

5. What was the official charge against Jesus? (27:37) In what way was it true?

6. What three groups taunt Jesus? (27:38-42) What do you think is the motivation for each group?

7. When have you or someone you care about been mocked? Why does it hurt so much?

8. The chief priests call on Jesus to save himself. (27:42) What would have happened if Jesus had saved Himself?

9. What does Jesus cry out in verse 46? What does it show about the depth of Jesus' isolation?

10. How does it make you feel to realize that Jesus went through this abuse alone for you?

27 Torn Curtain-Matt. 27:45-54

Pastor Bob was counseling Judy during the time of her divorce from Joe. Somehow, his help turned into an affair. After a month, Bob was racked with guilt. He went into the sanctuary and poured everything out about the affair and his troubled marriage to God. The guilt of it all was killing him. In that moment, he knew what he needed to do. He met with Judy and broke off the affair asking her to forgive him. He told his wife everything and begged for forgiveness. That weekend, he told the leaders of the congregation what he had done and asked for two weeks to take his wife for a marriage retreat. He would accept any punishment they wanted to give. He just needed to be right with God, his wife, and his church.

In writing to the Jews, Matthew included details that Jews would recognize as the hand of God. The darkness that began at noon (the sixth hour) would show creation crying out against the injustice of the cross. The earthquake would remind others of the trembling of Mt.

Sinai in Exodus 19. The dead rising would point to the effect that Jesus' cross would have on the last day. Yet, it was the tearing of the curtain in the temple that has the greatest significance. It shows that man is no longer separated from God by our sin. Jesus has paid for sin and brought man to God.

1. **When have you been separated from a loved one? What was that like?**

2. **What happened from the sixth to the ninth hour (noon to 3 PM) (27:45) What mood do you think that created around the cross?**

3. **What does Jesus cry out at the ninth hour? (27:46) What do you think His words meant?**

4. **When have you felt like God has forgotten you? How are God's words in Hebrews 13:5-6 a comfort to you at those times?**

5. What do the bystanders think Jesus shouted in verse 47? How does one person try to help Jesus?

6. With His lips now moist, Jesus cried out. Then what happened? (27:50) What does John's gospel (John 19:30) say that Jesus spoke?

7. How would you explain why it was necessary for Jesus to die to a non-Christian? What do you think life would be like for you if Jesus hadn't died?

8. What happened in the temple at the moment that Jesus died? (27:51) What was the purpose of this curtain in the temple?

9. What separates men from God today? How can we help others break down those walls?

10. The centurion saw all that had happened and declared Jesus was the Son of God (27:54) What have you seen or experienced that convinces you that Jesus is God?

29 Darkness turns to Joy-Matt 28:1-10

Her daughter Jill had been in an accident on the way to school. The officer on the phone didn't know any more than that the car was totaled and Jill was taken to Memorial Hospital. As Mary drove to the hospital, she cried and prayed and hoped that her daughter was still alive. She ran into the hospital and was taken to an emergency room where they were putting a cast on Jill's left arm. She was alive with a broken arm and a few bruised ribs. Embracing her daughter, Mary cried and never wanted to let go. The darkness had turned to joy. Thank you, Lord, for another miracle!

Early Easter morning, the women who had remained at the cross (Matt. 27:55-56) came bringing spices to finish the burial of Jesus. They had no thought of the resurrection and were not even sure how they would move the stone blocking the tomb's entrance (Mark 16:3). Yet their darkness would soon turn to joy. The story of Easter is the light in the life of every Christian. It separates those who only know about Jesus from those who believe in Him. It is the center of the Christian faith and the touchpoint of God's love for us.

1. **What was the saddest day you ever experienced? Who was there with you?**

2. **Who visits the tomb? (28:1) Why and when did they come?**

3. **What emotions do you think the women had that morning as they walked to the tomb?**

4. **What events had happened at the tomb before the women had come that morning? (28:2-4)**

5. **What news did the angel tell the women? (28:5)**

6. How did you come to know that Jesus had arisen? What convinced you that the account of His resurrection was true?

7. What command did the angel give the women (28:7) which Jesus repeats to them (28:10)?

8. Who is Jesus telling you to go and tell the news of the empty tomb?

9. How does Jesus show love for the women and His disciples (28:9-10)

10. How do the words of Jesus comfort and challenge you? What stands out to you in this account of the resurrection?

32 Disappointed with Easter?-Luke 24: 13-32

Janna hated going to church and Sunday school. The songs were old. She didn't know her Bible well enough to understand the pastor's sermons. All she knew was that church was about being good and helping people she didn't know. The only thing good about it was that Dad took them out for brunch after Sunday school. Then one Sunday, the service and Sunday school were led by a missionary from Africa. He started with a few Old Testament passages and opened up the Easter story as a story of joy. Christ was changing lives for those who knew Him. He finished the message by showing pictures of children like her smiling and digging a well so the village. Janna wanted that happiness and began searching the scripture and praying for it from that day. Now, living with Jesus has become her joy.

Two men were walking from Jerusalem to Emmaus, a village seven miles away, on the afternoon or early evening of Easter. The men heard accounts that Jesus was alive, but did not believe them. They were discouraged and disappointed as they discussed the events of Good Friday. They had high hopes for Jesus but found themselves frustrated that He had not been the Messiah that they sought. Many today have rejected Jesus because they have the wrong picture of Jesus. Jesus joins in the discussion and helps all of us understand who the Messiah really is.

1. **What dreams of yours have been broken? Who did you talk with about your broken dreams?**

2. **On Easter, two men are walking to Emmaus. How long is the trip to Emmaus and what do they talk about? (24:13-14)**

3. **How have the trials and disappointments of life and ministry affected you?**

4. What question does Jesus ask the two men? (24:17) How do the men describe the events of the last couple days and their hopes for the ministry of Jesus? (24:19-24)

5. What do you expect from the Christian life? How have you dealt with the times when you felt disappointed with God or with your life?

6. How does Jesus respond to the two men? (24:25) What does Jesus need to explain before He can reveal Himself to them? (24:26-27)

7. How well could you explain Jesus' death and resurrection to another person? What connection is there between our lack of understanding and a lack of faith in hard times?

8. When were the men allowed to see Jesus' true nature? (24:30-31) How had Jesus' teaching prepared them for this moment? (24:32)

9. When in your life have you come closest to giving up on ministry or on faith in God? What opened your eyes and strengthened your faith?

10. Why are we often "slow of heart to believe" (24:25)? What do you think Jesus would say to you and to your group if He walked down the road with you?

Leader's Guides

02 Love Stands Out-Mark 14:1-9

Angus McMahon stood tall with his wife at his side and his hands on the shoulders of two little girls. The mayor was reading a proclamation making this Angus McMahon day for this brave firefighter's rescue of the two girls who stood in front of him. When the girls beamed at him in the middle of the ceremony, Angus almost lost it. He felt their love and knew that he now had a connection to these two girls for the rest of their lives.

In the days before Palm Sunday, one woman shared her love with Jesus. John's gospel tells us that it was Mary, the sister of Lazarus who Jesus had raised from the dead. Pouring her perfume on Jesus' head filled the room with the scent of love. Her selfless act is criticized, but Jesus accepts her gift and defends her before the disciples. One wonders how much this act of love must have meant to Jesus as He entered the dark days to come. Mary teaches us to keep showing God's love even if others don't understand our gift.

1. **If you had fifty thousand dollars to spend on someone in your family, what would you buy?**

Answers will vary. Encourage the group to go wild and think of things that are outrageous. It may be an elaborate vacation or a motor home. It might be a party for all 200 of their extended relatives so the whole family can be together just once.

2. **When and where did the events of this story take place?** (14:1-3)

This story took place just days before Passover in the city of Bethany just outside of Jerusalem. Jesus had come to Bethany to stay with Mary, Martha, and Lazarus. Mark places this story between the two accounts of the desire to arrest Jesus to highlight the love of this woman. While the text doesn't name the woman, John's gospel tells us that she is Mary of Bethany, the sister of Lazarus and Martha (John 11). By placing this story between the accounts of the plot to arrest Jesus, Mark contrasted the treachery of Judas and the leaders with the love and loyalty of Mary.

3. **What amazing thing did a woman do while Jesus was visiting Bethany?** (14:3) **Why would this woman make this great a sacrifice for Jesus? (Hint: see John 11)**

This woman broke open a jar of expensive perfume and poured it on Jesus' head. An *alabaster jar* was a beautiful and expensive vase with a long, slender neck carved from translucent gypsum. This jar filled with pure ointment (nard) was purposely broken and poured on Jesus' head. Mary's gift to Jesus (a pint of this costly perfume, according to John 12:3-5) was worth a year's wages and filled the room with its fragrance. Three hundred denarii were the yearly wage paid for an average worker in Judea. The gift makes sense if you remember that this is only a few weeks after Jesus had raised Lazarus from the dead (John 11). Many of us would want to thank someone who only healed a close family member. Mary had been given back her brother and was expressing her love and appreciation for Jesus.

4.   What reaction did the woman's actions get? What was suggested as a better use for this gift? (14:4-5)

Mark says some of the disciples, but John specifically mentions Judas as being the one who was upset. The alternative that is mentioned was a charade to hide their true motives. They resented the gesture as a total waste of a large sum of money.

Judas may have also been greedy. As the treasurer of the

group, he was in control of the money and according to John

(John 12:6) had stolen money from the treasury of the disciples.

Mark's placement of this story may show that this event was

what pushed Judas over the edge so that he was willing to

betray Jesus.

5. **What extravagant thing would you like to do for Jesus if you had the money even if others might think is a waste?**

Answers will vary. It might be that you would like to have a large

organ in your church or a stain glass window. It might be that

you would like to have a single day when you feed the hungry

near your church or buy a bible for every kid in the

neighborhood. The things we feel passionate about are different

than the desires of others.

6. **Whom did Jesus rebuke? How did Jesus justify Mary's actions?** (14:6-8)

The disciples had missed the point and had made this woman

who had wanted to honor Jesus feel as if she had done

something wrong. Jesus rebukes the disciples and rises to the defense of Mary. He knew the heart of Mary and accepted what she had done. She had shown great love and appreciation for Jesus. He saw it as an act that would prepare Him for His burial and the events that were only a week or so away. There is a great lesson here in that we should not judge the good intentions of others even if it is not what we would have done in their place. Mary's motives were good and her heart was filled with love for Jesus.

7. What did Jesus predict? (14:9**) How did that make this a special opportunity to worship Jesus?**

Jesus tells them that His burial will soon be coming. The time for such devotion and anointing Jesus would soon be past. Jesus would soon be gone from them physically. One wonders if Mary, living so close to Jerusalem, was more aware of the dangers that Jesus might be facing as He attended this Passover. She may have wanted to show her appreciation before it was too late. Jesus' words on the poor do not disparage charity but were meant to highlight the special time as Holy Week drew near. They could feed the poor later, but His cross was coming soon.

8. **What do you think Jesus meant when He said: "She did what she could"? (**14:8**)**

Mary took the initiative. She used the resources that she had at hand and the opportunity she had to be with Jesus. While others often talked about doing something for Jesus, Mary actually did something special. Sometimes we may feel like we can't be a foreign missionary for Jesus or give a million dollar gift to the church. That may be true, but each of us has sacrifices and gifts that we can use for the Lord. We just need to find our gifts and use them.

9. **What can we learn about values from the woman in this story? (14:9)**

Mary's unselfish act will be remembered forever because the Lord chose to record her actions in scripture. While the disciples worried about what they saw as the best use of funds, Mary quietly loved Jesus and was so devoted to Him that she made the great sacrifice talked about in the text. Love given in a timely manner has power. We do what we are able to and don't wait for the perfect moment to show God's love. Give freely from your heart and you can change lives.

10. Mary was criticized for her act of selfless sacrifice.

What keeps you from showing your love for Jesus

and from making sacrifices for Him?

Answers will vary but may include a fear of criticism like Mary

received or busy lives that don't take the time to show the deep

love for Jesus. The point of the story is that we have the power

to change lives with the love of Jesus. Mary can inspire all of us

to show love for our Lord and for others. It will be remembered

by God and by those who we have touched. We just need to use

the resources that we have at hand and have the courage and

love for Jesus to make simple sacrifices.

03 What Did You Expect?-Luke 19:28-44

John had been the salesman of the year and so the company promoted him. Looking back, it seemed like the worst thing that they could have done to him. There were more pay and prestige, but now he was administering others and not doing the sales calls that he really loved and was successful at. The company had expectations of him that he struggled to reach. He had no experience running an office or managing others. He finally went to his boss and asked for his old job back. He just wanted to be the person God had made him.

Jesus comes riding into Jerusalem and the Passover amid the cheering of the crowds. Here was their Messiah and king. Surely, He would take up residence in Jerusalem and bring back Israel's glory. Sadly, the crowd didn't know Jesus. He was not the earthly king that they were looking for, but rather the savior that they needed. In the days ahead, Jesus would fulfill the ministry that the Father had given Him. Many would leave Jesus, but those who let Him be the Savior and Lord found a friend who would change their lives.

1. **What is your favorite part of a parade? Why do you think people like parades so much?**

Answers will vary. Some will love the bands (which are my favorite); others will love the floats especially if they throw candy or toys. Be sure to talk about when they last saw a parade and why people will stand for hours to get a good place to see a parade.

2. **Jesus starts out in Bethany. How close is this to Jerusalem? (19:29) What other events happened in Bethany?**

Bethany is on the southeastern slopes of the Mount of Olives and is about two miles east of Jerusalem close to the road that leads to Jericho. Bethany was the home of Mary and Martha where Jesus ate with His disciples (Luke 10:38-42) and the site of the raising of Lazarus (John 11). Jesus stayed in Bethany during the Passover and "commuted" into Jerusalem for the events of Holy Week.

3. **What instructions does Jesus give to two of the disciples? (19:30-31) What challenge does Jesus foresee?**

Jesus told two of the disciples to go into the village and bring an unridden colt to Jesus for His journey into Jerusalem. The directions seem a little cryptic, but remember that Jesus was nearing the cross and one of His disciples would betray Him. It would seem that Jesus

had made arrangements to borrow the colt. The plan had to be

quietly completed before the Jewish leaders knew what was

happening. The owners of the animal are not mentioned in

scripture, possibly because the Jewish leaders were

excommunicating anyone who confessed Jesus (John 9:22) and

may have wished to harm anyone who helped Jesus with His entry

into Jerusalem.

4. **When has Jesus given you a task that seemed**
    impossible? How did Jesus prepare you for the
    challenge?

Most Christians have been given tasks that they thought were

impossible. (The writing of this book has seemed at times

impossible for me). Encourage them to talk about the tasks that

seemed daunting and how the Lord does prepare us since He

wants us to succeed. In my case, this book came about because of

the Lord bringing a person named Rebecca who has a Christian

publishing house into my life. It could have never happened without

her help.

5. **How do you picture the scene in verses 35-38? If you**
    had been there, what sounds would you have heard and

what emotions would have been present in the people around you?

Answers will vary, but they might picture Jesus starting behind the hill traveling through people camped along the hill during the Passover celebration. Encourage them to hear the sounds and smells. Perhaps, a few people see Jesus at first and begin shouting. Perhaps, they can smell the campfires of the pilgrims or the smell of the animals. As they see Jesus, others drop what they are doing to come and stand along the sides of the road. First one person and then another puts their cloaks on the road. By the time that Jesus is going down the Mount of Olives, there is a large crowd shouting and pressing on one another to get a glimpse of Jesus riding down. The significance of His entry into Jerusalem coming like the Messiah would not have been lost on the crowd.

6. **What kind of reception do you think Jesus would get if He came to your town today?**

Answers will vary, but focus on how the people, the media, and the civic leaders would each react to Jesus. Also, ask how you think Jesus's presence would affect modern Christians and churches. Joseph Girzone has written an excellent book called *"Joshua"* that explores what it would be like if Jesus quietly came to our town today. I highly recommend the book if you want to explore this idea further.

7. **What do the people call Jesus as He entered the city? (19:38) What hopes or dreams of the people do those titles convey?**

The people call Jesus "king" and The expression "Blessed is the King who comes in the name of the LORD" may have been recited as part of the Passover tradition—as a blessing given by the people in Jerusalem to the visiting pilgrims (see Psalm 118:25-26). The people lined the road, praising God, waving branches, and throwing their cloaks in front of the colt as it passed before them. "Long live the King" was the meaning behind their joyful shouts because they knew that Jesus was intentionally fulfilling Old Testament prophecy. The people who were praising God for giving them a king had the wrong idea about Jesus. They expected him to be a national leader who would defeat the Romans and restore their nation to its former glory. They were deaf to the words of the Old Testament prophets and blind to Jesus' real mission. When it became apparent that Jesus was not going to fulfill their hopes, many would turn against him.

8. **What has God done for you recently that made you want to shout it out or tell others?**

This is a chance for a praise report. The crowd on Palm Sunday could easily have contained people who had been healed or who had listened to Jesus open up the scriptures for them. They had great hopes for the future with Jesus and much of that was based on His help from the past or what they knew of Jesus. The more we shout out how Jesus has helped us, the more we will impact others and help them to see Jesus as their hope.

9. **What do the Pharisees want Jesus to tell the crowd? (19:39) Why do you think that the Pharisees in the crowd are upset?**

The Pharisees practically order Jesus to rebuke the crowd and calm the people down. The Pharisees understood the Messianic undertones of the words of the crowd and thought that they were close to blasphemy. They also didn't want someone challenging their power and their comfortable reality. If the people called Jesus "king", it could lead to a revolt or to a reaction by the Roman governor and army. Jesus' answer recalls Habakkuk 2:11 where Habakkuk prophesies the judgment of God on Judah before the Babylonian captivity. If the praise for the Messiah was silenced, the walls of the city would bear witness to the city's rejection of God's servant.

10. What expectations do you have of Jesus? What do you want Him to come and bring into your life?

It is helpful to look at what we want from Jesus. Is Jesus just a savior from sin and hell? Is He someone that we pray to daily because we have come to rely on Jesus' help? (1 John 4:16) Christians have many expectations about who Jesus really is and what He brings to our lives. The purpose of this question is not to judge anyone's answers, but to help the group listen to each other and broaden their expectations of Jesus. He provides more for us than most of us ever think about.

06 The Joy of Serving-John 13 1-17

Pastor Bob looked around as he pulled up at the church on Sunday morning and noticed that the parking lot was full of snow. He went looking for the rusty orange shovel and finding it, began to shovel the sidewalks and the handicapped parking spots. One by one, the members of the church came. Tom had a shovel in his trunk and he began to help. Nancy swept the snow off the sidewalks near the building. Bill found some rock salt and began to spread it on the sidewalks so that they didn't refreeze. Soon, much of the parking lot was clear and the rest was passable. It was amazing how one person's example led them all to care for each other.

Jesus knew that Peter would deny Him and Judas would betray Him. He also knew that the disciples would all desert Him on His arrest. Yet, He wanted to show them the extent of His love and teach them a valuable lesson about service. He and the disciples were gathered in the upper room to celebrate the Passover Festival. As the meal began, no one had taken the time to wash the dirty feet of those who had come for the meal. Jesus showed that all of us are called to serve by taking a towel in order to wash and dry each of the disciple's feet. The lesson is simple. If He, the Son of God, is willing to serve such a lowly task, then there is no task that should be below any of us.

1. How beautiful are your feet? (Model ready, never looked, or feet like a troll)

Most of us never think about our feet unless they are somewhat troll-like. Have people rank their feet. For a fun activity in a small group have everyone take off their shoes and have the group vote on who has the prettiest and ugliest feet.

2. What does Jesus know that the disciples have not figured out? (13:1)

Jesus knew that "His hour was come." The cross was little more than 12 hours away as Jesus met with the disciples for the Passover Meal. More than any of the Gospel writers, John emphasized the fact that Jesus lived on God's timetable as He marched to the cross. Thus, John 13-17 will become Jesus' farewell message to his disciples. While many others in scripture had farewell messages (Moses, Joshua, and Paul for example), Jesus started with an object lesson that many of us will never forget.

3. Describe the scene in verses 3-5. What do you think

motivated Jesus to wash their feet?

Jesus wanted to take the opportunity to teach humility. The competitive spirit of the disciples would be on display in just a few minutes as they started an argument about who was the greatest (Luke 22:24-30). Here Jesus would give a lesson in humility that would show that selfishness and pride didn't belong in the church. It is important to see that Jesus did this out of love (13:1) and out of strength (13:3). Humility is not timidity, it is a concern for others even more than for yourself.

4. **Describe a person you know who has demonstrated unselfish service to others? What do you think makes them special?**

Answers will vary, but allow the members of the group to share stories about people who they have seen demonstrate unselfish service. Talk about the qualities that such people have so that the group might seek those qualities and values for their own lives. If it seems appropriate, pray about those qualities either now or at the end of this session asking the Holy Spirit to teach us and nurture us so that we have those qualities for our lives.

5. **How does Peter react to Jesus' service? (13:6-8) How does Jesus respond to Peter's refusal to be**

served?

Peter is often pictured at one end of the table. You can imagine Peter watching Jesus wash the other disciple's feet and becoming more and more disturbed as the Lord came near to him. Peter impulsively tells Jesus that the Master will never wash his feet. Peter was often impulsive in the gospels. He had opposed Jesus' prediction of the cross (Matt. 16:21-23) and spoke up at the transfiguration when he did not understand what was going on (Matt. 17:1-8). Sadly, Peter did not wait for an explanation, but again impulsively began telling Jesus what to do. First, he tells the Lord not to wash his feet. Then he tries to command Jesus to wash all of him as if that will make him closer to Jesus than any of the other disciples.

6. **How do you react when a superior unexpectedly serves you?**

Answers will vary, but usually, we feel uncomfortable and may even wonder what the boss' angle is. It is surprising in our world when a superior serves us, yet some of the greatest servants like Sister Theresa in India are admired for this kind of service. The point of Jesus' actions was to show that no service is below us. We should be willing to serve people who many would consider less than us.

7. **What does Jesus mean when He says, "Unless I wash you, you will have no part of me?" (13:8)**

Jesus' answer to Peter reflects our need for Jesus to wash away our sins on the cross. Those who live in their sin and refuse the cross can have no fellowship with Jesus. It is also important to let Jesus serve us every day. Only those who are forgiven and who depend on Jesus in prayer and in life will have Jesus and His blessings each day of their lives. Our lives are to be totally dependent on Jesus for every spiritual and material blessing.

8. **In what way does Jesus wash our feet today? What are the consequences of refusing Jesus' love and service?**

Answers may include answering our prayers, giving us forgiveness from the cross, or protecting us from the evil that is around us. It is important that we see that Jesus is still cleansing us from the cross and serving us every day. Discuss what life would be like if we didn't allow Jesus to perform these acts of service in our lives. Jesus does more for us each day than we often acknowledge. We are blessed by His great acts of service.

9. **How does Jesus challenge our ideas of leadership?**

(13:14-16) Why do we honor those who serve?

Jesus had just given them an example to follow. Happiness does not come from having others serve us, but from serving others in Jesus's name. Service elevates us and dignifies others. Yet, to know this truth was not enough. The disciples needed to put this into practice. They had honored Jesus for His years of humble service and He wanted them to give such service to others. People still honor those who selflessly serve. They watch these quiet servants changing lives and making the world around them better without worrying about themselves.

10. In what areas do you struggle to be humble? Who would benefit from your humble service today?

If the group has built a level of trust, let the members make confession of their areas of struggle. If the group has not reached that level, you might ask for examples of well-known people who struggle to be humble and how they affect the world around them. Close the session with each member of the group thinking about one person that they could serve in the next week. Challenge them to be specific about the person and one thing that they might do for that person.

09 The way to God-John 14:1-14

Whir. Whir. Whir. Each time that Larry tried to get out of the snowdrift, the tires spun even faster. He looked at Sandy and the kids and announced that he would walk back about a half mile to the convenience store to get help. Sandy looked at him, but before she could say a word, he said, "There is still plenty of light and it isn't that far. I'll be back for all of you very soon." With that, he began to walk away. True to his word, he was back in a half hour riding in a pickup truck. "This nice gentleman has a chain and will have us out in no time".

The section opens and ends with our Lord's comforting words, "Let not your heart be troubled." It should be no surprise that the disciples were struggling. Jesus had predicted Judas' betrayal (John 13:21) and Peter's denial (John 13:38). Yet the hardest words for the disciples to deal with were the words that Jesus was going to leave them (John 13:33). Questions circled their minds and fears began to take hold of them. Jesus would comfort them and let them know why He must go. Jesus assures all of us that heaven is a real place prepared for us and that He will come back and bring us there at the proper time.

1.   What is your greatest fear about the future?

Answers will vary a lot by age. The older the group, the more worries will probably be about health and retirement. A younger group may have worries about finding the right partner or job. Explore what the fears are and why they are so important to each person. Be careful not to discount someone's fear. It may seem "silly" to you, but it is important to them.

2.   What comfort does Jesus give His disciples? (14:2-3)

Jesus tells His disciples "do not let your hearts be troubled". We should not be surprised that the disciples felt "troubled" at that point. Jesus had announced that one of them was traitor, that Peter would deny his Lord three times and worst of all, that He was going to leave them (John 13:33) Questions swirled around them like mosquitos coming in for the kill. Where was He going (14:5) and perhaps could they go with Him? Jesus answer was that they should trust in God and trust in Him. (14:1)

3.   How does Jesus have your future covered? How is Jesus helping you with your life today?

This is a question about trust. As we listed all the fears that we have about the future, the question is whether we trust God to help us deal with those things and some things that we have not even begun to worry about? Perhaps one of the best ways to answer that question is to have the class list all the ways that God is helping us today and has helped us in the past. As we see the depth of God's love and help in our lives today, we learn to trust Him for tomorrow.

4. **What is Thomas' question to Jesus? (14:5) Put Jesus' answer in your own words? (14:6-7)**

Thomas asks how they can follow Jesus if they don't know where He is going. Thomas had already shown an intense desire to be with Jesus even if it meant that the disciples would die with Jesus. (John 11:16) Jesus' answer shows that He is going to the Father and they He is the only way to God. The knowledge that Jesus was preparing a place for them would help them overcome the obstacles along the way. Jesus also promised that they will know and see God. They will see things that will help them to put their trust in God in the years ahead.

5. **How is Jesus the way and truth in your life? (14:6)**

Jesus is not a way to heaven. He is the only way since people come to God only through the cross. This question asks how we are showing our trust in Jesus in our lives. Jesus wipes away our need for good works to earn heaven. His cross is our only way. All other ways are false and do not lead us truthfully. His way alone will lead us to eternal life. How do the members of the group depend on Jesus and in what ways do they stand up for Jesus in a world where all ways are viewed as equal?

6. What question does Jesus ask the disciples? (14:9)

Jesus asks Philip if he really knows Him since they have been together for so long. The question begs for an answer of Yes. Philip should have known that Jesus words and actions had come from the God. As one of the twelve, Philip had seen miracles of healing, demons cast out, and the wind calmed in a way that only God could do. He had heard Jesus open up the scripture and teach them with power. In many ways, these disciples had been closer to God than even Abraham or Moses.

7. What tone of voice do you imagine Jesus speaking to His disciples? How does Jesus speak to you when you want your own way?

Answers will vary, but I picture Jesus disappointed and perhaps frustrated at the same time that He was showing his great love for these men. Other answers are possible and you should encourage people to speak what is on their hearts and not to criticize each other. God still speaks to us through prayer and His word, the Bible.

God can also speak to us through situations and through other Christians. How God speaks is not as important as seeing that He still speaks to us and helps us through our doubts and concerns.

8. How would you respond to someone who says there are many ways to God?

Answers will vary and a good discussion could ensue. Jesus' answer "I am the way" in verse 6 excludes the many ways that our society wants to make equal. If asked, I personally have found it unhelpful to argue with people. I prefer to just to tell them how Jesus alone has helped me and to mention all the ways that I have been loved by Jesus. You may wish to ask the person how they plan to get to God. Many will not have a way and you can share that Jesus is your way and that you would be glad to help them come to Him and know Him.

9. What promise does Jesus make to those who have faith in Him? (14:12-13)

Jesus promises that His followers will be able to do the things that He has been doing. They will change lives by sharing His teaching and will see miraculous answers to prayer. Powerful prayer is based on trust in God and can truly work miracles. The disciples in the book of Acts will heal the sick, raise the dead and speak before crowds and kings. Those who have faith will have powerful prayers and will have the ability to speak on Jesus' behalf as His ambassador before many people as well. As for the "greater part", we need to remember that Peter alone spoke before the crowd on Pentecost and had 3000 come to faith in one day. The depth of power that Christians have been given by Jesus is truly amazing.

10. What greater things do you want to ask God to let you do with your life? How would those ministries impact others?

This is your chance to dream big. Our temptation is to think small, but the sky is literally the limit with God at our side. Dream about doing a mission trip or about impacting those in your family who do not believe. Let the knowledge of how such ministry can impact others be the motivation to pray for your opportunity from the Lord. God wants people to try big things and use His power to change lives.

13 Be Transformed With Joy-John 16:16-33

Jamie was sick and tired of being pregnant. She waddled into every room and found it hard to find anything that fit. She just felt tired of feeling fat. Surely, having the baby would be easier. Then the night of the delivery came. As she sweated and strained with every push, she hated her husband and wished she had never gotten pregnant. Suddenly, delivery was over and the nurse put her little girl into her arms. Jamie immediately forgot about all the pain and looked into the blue eyes straining to stare at her. She looked forward to a lifetime of getting to know and love this child that God had brought into her life.

As Jesus concluded His teaching with the disciples on Thursday night, He dealt with their emotions. They were sad, confused and afraid because of what He had said to them. He brought them a message of joy. While they were definitely not feeling joyful that night, He promised that the events that lie ahead would turn their sorrow to joy. It would be a joy that would come from inside as the Holy Spirit helped them understand and gave them faith. The disciples were real men and faced the same kind of struggles that we often have. Their struggles remind us that we can have that same kind of joy, too.

1. **What was your most difficult or confusing class in school? What emotions rise up in you as you think of that class?**

Answers will vary. Focus on the anxiety and fear that certain subjects gave each of us. Let them gain that feeling even as they look at the anxiety the disciples were feeling at this supper that should have been a time of celebration and joy.

2. **What is Jesus referring to in verse 16? What tone do you hear in the disciples' voices in verses 17-18?**

It is easy for us to look back through the crucifixion and resurrection and understand what Jesus means when He says that they would not see him for a little while after He was buried and then see Him again on Easter. It may be that Jesus is also talking about his ascension. After the ascension, they would not see Him, but would know that he was with them. On the last day, when we all rise from the dead, we will see Jesus again and live with Him in heaven. There may be many answers about what the tone of their discussion would have been like, but certainly, there was fear and confusion. They want to ask Him what He meant but were afraid to do so. They ask the questions of each other, but no one seemed to have the answers.

3. **How do you deal with confusing passages in scripture?**

Answers will vary, but may include ignoring them, being bothered about them or praying about them. They may also come to their pastor or to someone who seems to know the Bible better. As a challenge to the class, you might want to ask them what they would have done if they had been one of the disciples or what passages are confusing or challenging to them.

4. **What is Jesus' explanation in verse 20? Looking at Good Friday and Easter, how did His words come true?**

Jesus tells them that they will weep and mourn while the world rejoices, but that their grief will turn to joy. On Good Friday, the Pharisees and Sadducees were probably celebrating. The upstart rabbi who had been such a problem would soon be dead and out of their hair. Meanwhile, the disciples were afraid up in the upper room and thought that their world was ending. Easter changed all that as the risen Lord appeared to the disciples and brought joy to their hearts. (Luke 24:40-41) The guard's report of the empty tomb and the angel rolling back the stone (Matthew 28:2-4, 11-12) must have caused panic among the chief priests.

5. **What analogy did Jesus use to further explain His departure? (16:21) In what ways does the woman feel pain and joy in childbirth?**

To help them understand, Jesus used the analogy of a mother with a newborn child. During the birthing process, the mother will have great pain. When she holds that baby in her arms for the first time, she forgets about the pain and is filled with such love and joy because of the newborn child. In the same way, Good Friday and Holy Saturday would be times of great pain and anguish, but the joy of Easter would wipe away the tears from their eyes. Oddly, the pain of Good Friday was necessary if the joy of Easter was to be theirs.

6. **When have you felt pain as you served others? How did God bring joy in that situation?**

Answers will vary but may include physical pain as we did something strenuous like work in a soup kitchen all day or emotional as we sat with someone who just found out they had cancer crying on our shoulder and asking for answers. Yet, God often gives us a feeling of purpose and joy as we make a difference in someone's life by the work that we did. There may also be times where the joy and the answers that we seek in those painful times will have to wait for months or years or possibly when we reach heaven. These have been times where I served someone and found no joy other than knowing that I had served the Lord and represented Him well.

7. **What power have the disciples not unlocked? (16:23-24) What promises are made about the power of prayer in these verses?**

As we will see in the Garden of Gethsemane (Matt. 26:36-46) where the disciples sleep rather than pray, the disciples had not unlocked the power of prayer. They had been afraid to ask Jesus for answers (16:18-19), but will one day not be afraid to bring their needs to the Father. (16:26) The heart of this promise is that the Father loves them and that He wants to hear their requests and meet their needs. Jesus had taken care of them on earth. Now they would turn to the Father and He would provide. Jesus was leaving, but they would not be left alone.

8. **How is the relationship to the Father described? (16:27) How is our relationship with God the key to joy?**

The relationship with the Father is one of love. Nowhere does it say that we must love Him first. God has always loved us and has shown that love in the cross where He gave His son for us. Our faith relationship with God opens the doors for us to feel and to live in that love. Joy comes into our lives because we know that we have a God who loves us and cares for us. The more time we spend in Bible study and prayer getting to know the Lord, the more confident that we will be coming to Him in prayer and the more open we will be to the blessings that He wants to bring into our lives.

9. **How well do you deal with change? How have the challenges and pains of life helped you grow?**

Sometimes we deal with change by ignoring it or refusing to make the change. Other times, we may have changes like going to college or getting married that we are eager to make. The disciples' lives would change drastically overnight. They would go from being followers of Jesus to martyrs who died for their faith. Change may be hard for us, but we often learn by the challenges. We would question most people who stay living at their parents' home when they are 45 or wear the bell bottom pants of high school. We have to adjust and change. The good news is that God will be with us every step of the way.

10. What is the difference between the joy promised by the world and the joy promised by Jesus?

The joy of the world is all about temporary pleasure and happiness. We do things that will make us happy like going on a great trip or winning an award. Yet, the joy doesn't last for we have to return to school or to a job after vacation. Jesus's joy is different. It transforms us and will be with us for life. The mother who gives birth to her first born child will be a changed person because of the joy that she has in the child. Christians are transformed by the joy of Jesus. They still face the same pains that the world does, but they have a loving savior who they can talk to in prayer and who they can believe in as the one who will help them. With Jesus, we never walk alone.

16 Broken Sanctuary-Luke 22:39-48

It had been a brutal three weeks. The Parkinson deal had drained everything out of Tom. He had come to Estes Park for a few days off. He drove up to Bear Lake so he could hike the trail to Emerald Lake. He let the trail push the last couple days away and reconnect him with memories of hiking this trail with his dad. Sitting on the edge of Emerald Lake, he glanced at Hallett Peak and began to pray about God's greatness. Shortly before sunset, he slowly walked down to Bear Lake. As he drove back to the hotel, his cell phone started chirping. He knew that something had gone wrong back at work. His quiet vacation had been interrupted.

Having spent the evening with the disciples at the last supper, Jesus wanted sanctuary before He faced the cross. He came to Gethsemane and began to pray. Here was a place where He could find quiet and time to be with the Father. Wrapped in the arms of the Father, He drew comfort and courage for what lay ahead. As we face struggles, it is nice to know that we have the sanctuary of prayer as well.

1. **Where do you go when you want to be alone and think? What makes that place special?**

Answers will vary, but might include a quiet place in the house, a park or a special place like Rocky Mountain National Park was for Tom in our story. The place may be special because of a memory or just because it is close and "safe".

2. **What does this passage reveal about Jesus's habits? (Luke 22:39) Why is time at Gethsemane important to Jesus as He prepares for the cross?**

Jesus was in the habit of coming to this place to pray and be with His disciples. It was so familiar that Judas knew to look for Jesus in this place (John 18:2). Jesus depended on prayer throughout His ministry. He has come here to be with the Father at a time when He needs the Father more than ever. The hours that He would spend here would strengthen Him for the task ahead. He poured out His emotions even as He submits to the Father's will.

3. **What does Jesus ask the disciples to pray for? (Luke 22:40) Why was such a prayer so important?**

Jesus asks the disciples to pray that they would not be overcome by temptation. He would soon be taken from them. They would need strength to face the temptation to run away or deny their faith. They would see Jesus die and find many of their hopes dashed. They could easily doubt everything that He had told them. It would be only by the strength of the Father and the Spirit that they would keep their faith and push aside the temptations that Satan would bring upon them.

4. **Jesus prays "yours (will) be done" in verse 42. What does Jesus' prayer reveal about His own character and His relationship with the Father?**

Jesus speaks his true feelings as a man. He knows that Judas is already meeting with the Jews to plan His arrest. He knew the price He would pay for bringing salvation to men. This was the cup that the man Jesus didn't want to drink. Yet, He reaffirmed His desire to do what God wanted. In this one sentence, we see both the terrible suffering and the total obedience of the Son to God's mission of salvation. The time for sanctuary is short.

5. **When you find yourself in a difficult situation, do you pray for deliverance or for strength to do what is right? What is the difference and what did Jesus pray for?**

Encourage them to be honest with this question. We often pray for deliverance from any kind of pain or suffering. We want an easy way out. What Jesus prays for here is the strength to do the Father's will.

He knows that doing what God wants will not be easy because He understands the full effect of His upcoming death on the cross. Yet, the easy way out for Jesus would have condemned us to eternal punishment. He knew that He would have to die to save us. The easy way out is not always the best and so we need to pray for God's will and not our ease.

6. **What does this passage tell us about Jesus' physical and emotional condition shortly before His death? (22:44) How was Jesus strengthened at this difficult time? (22:43)**

Luke the physician is the only gospel writer that mentions "sweat like drops of blood". By describing with the word "like" he may be describing sweat dropping heavily to the ground or a condition that results from the rupturing of blood vessels due to great emotional stress. Luke wants us to see how difficult this was for Jesus. Luke also is the only writer to mention God sending an angel to strengthen Jesus. It was obvious that the Heavenly Father noticed how difficult it was for Jesus and graciously gave Him encouragement and help as He faced this task.

7. **What would times of regular prayer bring to your life when you face painful or difficult times?**

Answers will vary, but the point is that we have someone who has demonstrated His love for us again and again. If we think about all the ways that God has helped us, we would never doubt that He always has our best interests at heart. Jesus had told the disciples to take time for prayer (22:40) as they entered the garden. As we experience troubles and temptations, God should be the first one that we seek and not the last. He alone can protect and help us through difficult times and provide us answers to our troubles.

8. **What did Jesus find the disciples doing when He returned to them? (22:45) What was the reason for their exhaustion?**

Matthew's gospel records that Jesus went back to the disciples several times finding them asleep each time. He needed their support in prayer for the task ahead was hard. Their exhaustion was probably a combination of a long day and Jesus' words about His departure from them (John 13:33). He had taught them a lot around the Last Supper table which could have easily left them emotionally exhausted. Sadly, their lack of prayer would be their undoing. Without God's strength, they would all flee and leave Jesus to face His accusers alone.

9. **How do Jesus' actions and attitudes compare to the**

disciples in this time of crisis? Which are more effective
and why?

Jesus spends hours with the Father in prayer, was strengthened by
God and would stand tall through the arrest, the trials, and even the
cross. The disciples would run and hide with only one disciple even
showing his face at the cross. Prayer was Jesus' fortress as it gave
Him power from above. The disciples were exhausted and slept.
One wonders how the story would have changed if they had spent
even a fraction of the time that Jesus spent in prayer.

**10. What does Jesus teach us in Gethsemane about the
sanctuary of prayer? What is one area in your life where
prayer could bring greater peace?**

At the Last Supper, Jesus prepared the disciples for what lay ahead.
Here in the Garden of Gethsemane, Jesus prepared Himself for the
trial and the cross. We often tackle big projects without prayer.
Jesus prayed before He chose the twelve disciples (Luke 6:12) and
was transfigured after a time of prayer (Luke 9:28). He sought
refreshment in prayer after healing a large number of people (Luke
4:42) and taught parables on prayer (Luke 18:1). Luke's gospel, in
particular, describes many times when Jesus left the ministry and
disciples behind in order to take the time to pray. Such strength and

help can be ours as well in this gift from God. Have each person commit either verbally or have them write down one area that they will pray about this week. If your situation allows it, you might consider beginning your next Bible study with "prayer reports" that tell how the prayers helped the participants.

18 Don't give in to evil-Mark 14:53-65

Frank was having a great night with his friends. The group had gone to the movies and now were just hanging out at the mall. They went into the dime store and Tim challenged them all to try to shoplift a small item for fun. Frank was horrified and told them that he wouldn't do it. Not only that, he would rat them out as they left the store. His buddies grumbled and shot angry glances at him as they left the store empty handed. The man at the cash register stopped the group and thanked Frank and then pointed to the cameras on the ceiling. "You just saved your buddies some jail time."

Having been arrested, Jesus was brought to the house of Caiaphas so that the chief priests could find evidence and make their case against Jesus. The "trial" was filled with false evidence that didn't match. Finally, the high priest asks Jesus to incriminate himself in violation of Jewish law. Jesus is a model for all of what to do when evil attacks. He is quiet when the room is filled with lies but is not afraid to answer to the truth. Don't give in to evil, but keep your character so that the Lord can protect you.

1. What injustice do you see in our society?

Answers will vary but may include a greedy politician or children who are starving. To start things off, you might want to bring newspaper articles and have the group discuss what makes the acts in the newspaper an injustice and how society should deal with it.

2. Who was gathered together (14:53) and what was their purpose? (14:55)

After a preliminary trial at Annas' home (mentioned only in John 18:12f), Jesus is taken to the home of Caiaphas, the current high priest. The language suggests that this was a trial by the Sanhedrin. The trial had two parts. First, they met at Caiaphas' home to gather evidence. Then they had an official trial in the temple as soon as it was daylight.

3. What perversions of justice do you see in this "trial"? (14:55-61)

Several actions were illegal according to Jewish law and custom. First, this trial was being held at night outside the normal court (14:53). Second, the group was gathering evidence and could not make their statements agree (14:56). Honest people would have concluded that Jesus was innocent. Third, the high priest asks a question meant to get Jesus to incriminate Himself (14:61) The Jews thought that they had Jesus in their control and they were determined to get rid of Him as soon as possible.

4. Why do you think Jesus remained silent as these accusations were made? (14:61)

There seemed to be no shortage of witnesses that night, but none could agree. Jesus wisely let the people make their conflicting accusations. It must have unnerved the chief priests to see Jesus quietly letting them destroy their own evidence. The Law of Moses decreed that no one could be put to death unless there were two or more witnesses. (Deut. 19:15) Jesus sat silently and let the Jews defeat themselves.

5. How do you act when someone accuses you? Why do you feel compelled to react this way?

Answers may vary, but many of us immediately proclaim our innocence. Explore the reactions of the group and ask why so many people act differently than Jesus. You might also explore what gave Jesus the confidence to remain quiet while the world seemed against Him and what makes us want to defend ourselves.

6. **What does the high priest ask in order to force Jesus to speak? (14:61) How does Jesus answer? (14:62)**

Caiaphas, the High Priest asks Jesus point blank if He is the Christ. Matthew's gospel (Matt. 26:63) tells us that Caiaphas had called Jesus to answer under oath this question so that Jesus was forced to answer according to Jewish law. It was an illegal move, but Caiaphas was not above skewing justice if he could get the evidence that he needed. Jesus had not bothered answering the false evidence, but to not answer this question would have seemed as if He was denying who He was. His answer, "I am" not only answers the question but points to Jesus' divinity for "I Am who I am" is what God called Himself before Moses in Exodus 3:14.

7. **Jesus went on to say, "And you will see the Son of Man sitting at the right hand of the Mighty One and coming on the clouds of heaven." (14:62) What is Jesus predicting will happen on the last day? How will the High Priest feel then?**

Jesus is referring to Daniel 7: 13-14 where "one like the Son of Man" was given authority over all the people. Jesus is predicting a great role reversal. In this courtroom, the Jews presume to judge Him, but on the last day, it will be Jesus who will judge them. Jesus is asserting His deity and presents a very scary picture for all those in the room. The high priest and the others should be shaking in their boots for they will face nothing but terror on the last day when they see an almighty Jesus at the right hand of God the Father.

8. **Why did the High Priest tear his clothes? (14:63) What did they feel was blasphemous about Jesus's statement?**

The high priest tore his clothes because Jesus had just claimed to be "I am". In his mind, this lawbreaker had just claimed to be God and was surely leading people astray. If anyone else had made that claim, it would have been blasphemy and punishable by death. We know the truth that Jesus is God and that He will be the one sitting at God's right hand judging all men. His words about being God and the prediction that they would see the Son of Man on the last day should have brought repentance. Instead, they brought anger.

9. **What punishment did the chief priest pronounce on Jesus? (14:64) How did the Jews show their disdain for**

Jesus? (14:65)

Blasphemy was punishable by death according to Leviticus 24:16. Jesus had just given them all the evidence that they needed. No more witnesses would be called for because their witnesses were worthless anyway. While they should have recognized Jesus as a great prophet (for no one else could do miracles as He had done), they were blind and refused to listen to His teachings or judge them by scripture. Instead, they showed their disdain for this "false prophet" by spitting on Him and striking Him with their fists.

10. How does Jesus' behavior differ from the behavior of the chief priests and elders? What can you learn from Jesus about dealing with those who oppose you?

The Jews had their minds made up before they came to the trial. They tried to use lies, intimidation and fear against Jesus. Jesus remained silent to all the false accusations and spoke only when silence would seem like a denial of the truth. They were angry and Jesus was calm. They were out of control and Jesus was totally in control of the situation. Jesus is an example of patience, calmness and confidence for us when we find ourselves dealing with people who oppose us. Like Him, we must trust God in these difficult situations. If there is time, ask the class how they might implement what Jesus has taught us. It is one thing to know what to do and another to have a strategy to do it.

21 Looking for loopholes - Luke 23:1-25

My twenty-something adult children for years insisted that my wife and I have an Easter egg hunt for them as we did when they were children. It had been our custom to hide a few eggs with money in it. I thought that this should be the last year for Easter egg hunts and so I put an IOU in one of the eggs. "This certificate good for five dollars except in the states of Kentucky, Ohio, Indiana, and Illinois". I thought I had the kids because those were all the states we regularly visited. Three years later, I was proven wrong. We were visiting West Virginia and my son pulled the certificate out of his wallet and requested his five dollars. I guess not every loophole can stand the test of time.

We know Pilate's name from the Apostle's Creed. He was the governor of Judea for about ten years. His word was law and the Romans were in full control of Palestine. Yet, he will be remembered as the man who tried Jesus and knew that Jesus was innocent, but sent Him off to the cross anyway. He is afraid of the Jews and tries to do the right thing in the wrong way. Instead of just proclaiming Jesus to be innocent, Pilate tries to find a loophole that will get both Jesus and Pilate off the hook. It doesn't work.

1. **What do you think it would be like to be on trial? How would it affect your life and your family?**

Answers will vary but have them imagine what it would be like to have witness after witness speak against them. Imagine how the threat of a long prison sentence would impact their life and lives of their family. How might it make a difference if you knew that you were innocent? Have the group put themselves in Jesus' position as much as possible.

2. **What is the charge against Jesus before Pilate? (23:2) How is this charge different than the charge that the Sanhedrin made? (see Mark 14:64)**

The Jewish leaders found Jesus guilty of blasphemy (Mark 14:64), but that charge would be meaningless in a Roman court and so they presented Jesus as a rebel who was subverting the Roman government. He was accused of being a king who told people not to pay their taxes. The Jews wanted Jesus executed on a cross so that the Romans would be seen as being at fault for His death. The irony is that these Jewish leaders hated Pilate and he hated them, yet they were forced to come to him since they could not carry out the death penalty.

3. **What is Pilate's first question to Jesus? (23:3) Why do you think Pilate determined Jesus was innocent even though Jesus admits that He is a king?**

Pilate's question, "Are you the King of the Jews?" focuses on the accusation of Jesus claiming to be a king since that would be an act of treason. Bound and beaten (Luke 22:63-65), Jesus did not look much like any king that would be a threat to Pilate. If this king was treated this badly by the Jewish leaders, He surely would not be a threat to Rome. The Jews might claim that Jesus was a king, but Jesus did not seem to have much of a following.

4. **Sometimes Jesus is silent before His accusers, sometimes He speaks. What do you learn from Jesus about how to respond to your accusers?**

Answers will vary, but Jesus always seems to be quiet when the accusations are false. If the accusations are true (even when, like Pilate, the person does not fully understand the statement's truth), Jesus will answer and acknowledge the truth. One thing that stands out to me is that we should ignore the lies about us, but need to acknowledge when people tell the truth even if it might be easier to keep quiet at those times as well. Keeping silent when the truth is spoken can lead people to false impressions as much as a lie can.

5. The Jews feel Jesus slipping away from their hands. What charge do they make to persuade Pilate? (23:5)

In desperation, they trump up more charges. Jesus never caused riots in his ministry. It was ironic that these men who hated the influence that Jesus had with the people would accuse Him of having such great powers over the crowds. It was a charge that Pilate had to take seriously since he was charged with keeping the peace. It was also a charge that Pilate knew had to be false or he would have heard about the riots of this Jesus from his spies across the countryside.

6. Why was Herod anxious to see Jesus? (23:8) How serious a threat does Herod think Jesus really is?

This was the Herod who had killed John the Baptist (Mark 6:26-28). He had heard about Jesus miracles and had longed to see Jesus (Luke 9:9). Now he had the opportunity to see Jesus for himself and hoped that Jesus would do some miracle as a way of influencing Herod to release Him. To Herod, Jesus was a traveling magician of some kind. Ironically, while Jesus speaks to Pilate and to Caiaphas, He says nothing to Herod when Herod questions Jesus. Herod had not listened to John and so it seems that Jesus had nothing more to say to Herod.

7. **Having failed to wash his hands of Jesus by sending Him to Herod, how does Pilate try to reason with the Jews (23:15-16)**

Having failed to get rid of the problem of Jesus, Pilate finds that he must make a decision before these Jewish leaders cause a riot. The Jewish leaders had hoped for a quick verdict on Jesus and had instead watched Jesus be shuffled to Herod and now back to Pilate. Time was being wasted when they wanted to prepare for the Passover. Pilate attempted to persuade them that Jesus was innocent of the charges. Pilate saw a poor and beaten man who seemed hardly to be one capable of the things that the Jews had accused Him of. He even appeals to Herod's decision of innocence (23:15) hoping that Herod's verdict might persuade them.

8. **Why is it difficult to reason with unjust people?**

Answers may vary, but it is obvious in this case that the Jews had their minds made up before they came. They knew that the charges were a hoax, but hated Jesus so much that they wanted Him dead. People often don't want justice but want their way. If you have the opportunity, discuss a recent account of injustice from the news. Let the group discuss how they would handle someone who could not be reasoned with.

9. What is Pilate's desire for Jesus? (23:22) In what way did the crowds influence Pilate's actions?

Pilate wants to release Jesus. Matthew tells us that Pilate's wife had experienced a dream (Matt. 27:19) about Jesus which probably scared a superstitious Roman like Pilate. He began to try to bargain with the crowd which threatened him that he was no friend of Caesar if he let Jesus go (John 19:12). The fate of Jesus was in Pilate's hands alone. He could have released Jesus and the crowd could not overrule the sentence. Yet the crowd protested and Pilate gave in. He sacrificed Jesus to save himself.

10. When do you find it hardest to stand up to the crowd? What would you have done in Pilate's place?

Let the group discuss how much of an influence others have on them. We would all like to think that we would have had the courage to stand up to the crowd if we were Pilate, but I for one must admit that I am not sure if I would have done the right thing. In Pilate's eyes, Jesus was not important to Pilate and thus was disposable. He surely would not have guessed how significant the man standing before him really was.

24 Forsaken – Cross-Matt. 27:32-50

Tammy went to a party at a friend's house and ended up pregnant with a boy that she barely knew. As the pregnancy started showing, people began to treat her differently. Many of her friends kept their distance. A young man that she liked would have nothing to do with her. Even her parents refused to talk about how she was going to finish High School with a newborn. Finally, an older woman named Thelma at her church took Tammy under her wing. She helped Tammy create her own plan for finishing High School and even for going on to get her associate's degree. She talked with Tammy's mom about the plans and even volunteered to watch the baby twice a week. She was the one true friend that Tammy had during this dark time in her life.

In His last hours, Jesus received very little comfort or support. Having faced six trials through the night and early morning and been beaten by Jew and Roman alike, Jesus is expected to carry his cross. He cannot do it and a stranger is enlisted for the task. The Romans took His clothes and the Jews stood before the cross and made fun of Him. Only one of His disciples dared to come to the cross (John 19:25-27) and the women watched from a distance (verses 55-56). When we feel lonely or lost, we know that we can turn to Jesus.

1. **Describe a time you felt all alone? What would it have meant to have a friend by your side?**

Answers will vary but focus on the feelings and emotion of that time. Jesus was all alone on the cross and this exercise can help us understand what it was like for Him to be forsaken. Likewise, the second question reminds us of the support that one special person can give – a support that Jesus was denied.

2. **Who is forced to carry Jesus' cross? (27:32) Why does Jesus need this help?**

His name is Simon and he was from Cyrene in North Africa. The gospel of Mark (Mark 15:21) adds that he was "the father of Alexander and Rufus". Since the gospel of Mark was going to the Romans and Paul mentions a Rufus (Romans 16:13), it may be that Simon's actions of carrying the cross led to his conversion to the faith. If you consider the beating that Jesus took at the hands of the Jews (Matthew 26:67) and again from the Romans (Matt. 27:27-31), it is easy to see why Jesus was in no shape to carry the heavy cross.

3. **Having nailed Jesus to a cross, what do the soldiers do with his possessions? (27:35-36)**

Contrary to the modest artwork we are used to seeing, Jesus would have been hanged virtually naked. The Romans considered His garments part of their spoil and divided them between the soldiers. They even gambled over the choicest piece (John 19:23).

4. **What do you think it was like being hung naked in a public place for hours?**

Living in a nation where even the worst criminals have rights, we struggle to understand the humiliation that Roman crucifixion was meant to be. Each criminal hung on a cross to slowly and painfully die. It was an advertisement to the people that they should not cross the Roman government. The extent of the pain and the humiliation of the cross were meant to deter crime. Once the Romans found you guilty, you had very few civil rights.

5. **What was the official charge against Jesus? (27:37) In what way was it true?**

The official charge (which the Jews had brought against Jesus in Luke 23:2) was that of being a king. John 19:20 tells us that the charge was written in three languages so that anyone coming to

Jerusalem could read the charge. The Jews felt Pilate was mocking them and protested the sign (John 19:21). If this stripped and executed man was truly the king of the Jews as the Jewish leaders had claimed, His execution would be seen as an insult every Jew. The truth of the sign was simple. As Messiah, Jesus was the king of His people. He was dying for them that they might have freedom and the opportunity to be children of God. Jesus even claimed that He was born to be a king (John 18:37) in His discussion with Pilate.

6. What three groups taunt Jesus? (27:38-42) What do you think is the motivation for each group?

Jesus will be mocked by the two robbers on either side of Him (27:38, 44), the crowd passing by (27:39) and the Jewish leaders (27:41-43). Let the group put themselves in the shoes of each group and find the motive they would have had in their place. One suggestion would be that the robbers mocked Him because here was the only one that they considered in a worse situation than they were. The crowd passing by got caught up in the spirit of things and mocked Him for fun. The Jewish leaders surely mocked Jesus out of hate. They had Jesus where they wanted Him and were enjoying the opportunity to pay Him back for the trouble that He had been.

7. **When have you or someone you care about been mocked? Why does it hurt so much?**

Let the class relate their stories. Mocking by itself seems to do no physical harm but causes deep scars emotionally as it changes how we see ourselves and changes the relationships that all of us need to survive. We often think that it was easy for Jesus on the cross because He was God, yet He was also a man and would have felt the loneliness and the insults very deeply.

8. **The chief priests call on Jesus to save himself. (27:42) What would have happened if Jesus had saved Himself?**

Jesus had saved many during His ministry including raising people like Jairus' daughter and Lazarus from the dead. The Jewish leaders taunt Him to save Himself (27:42). Could He have saved Himself? Surely He could have. Jesus had explained to Pilate that His servants would have fought to save Him if His kingdom were of this world (John 18:38). It is hard to believe that He could not have called down for a legion of angels if He had truly wanted to be free. Yet, to save Himself would have meant to doom us. Someone has to pay for sin and Jesus offered Himself freely so that we might have salvation.

9. **What does Jesus cry out in verse 46? What does it show about the depth of Jesus' isolation?**

Jesus' cry of My God, My God, why have you forsaken me?" is not one of despair but is a quote from Psalm 22:1. The psalm speaks of the isolation as God is "so far from saving me", but quickly turns to the fact that God is enthroned as the Holy One (Psalm 22:3) who delivered those who trusted in Him (Psalm 22:4). Jesus knew that God would not be able to look upon His Son the moment that Jesus took our sin upon Himself, but that the victory of the resurrection was the deliverance for those who trusted in the Father. Thus those words echo the pain of the cross and the hope of salvation for those who trust in the Lord.

10. **How does it make you feel to realize that Jesus went through this abuse alone for you?**

The cost of the cross was great, but so is our salvation. Let the class focus on the sacrifice that Jesus made for us and the love that drove Him to our cross. As we look at the cross, we need not feel guilty. We should feel honored and loved because our Savior would do this for us. The gospels paint a picture of the cross without being bloody as they show the pain and suffering endured for all of us.

27 Torn Curtain-Matt. 27:45-54

Pastor Bob was counseling Judy during the time of her divorce from Joe. Somehow, his help turned into an affair. After a month, Bob was racked with guilt. He went into the sanctuary and poured everything out about the affair and his troubled marriage to God. The guilt of it all was killing him. In that moment, he knew what he needed to do. He met with Judy and broke off the affair asking her to forgive him. He told his wife everything and begged for forgiveness. That weekend, he told the leaders of the congregation what he had done and asked for two weeks to take his wife for a marriage retreat. He would accept any punishment they wanted to give. He just needed to be right with God, his wife, and his church.

In writing to the Jews, Matthew included details that Jews would recognize as the hand of God. The darkness that began at noon (the sixth hour) would show creation crying out against the injustice of the cross. The earthquake would remind others of the trembling of Mt. Sinai in Exodus 19. The dead rising would point to the effect that Jesus' cross would have on the last day. Yet, it was the tearing of the curtain in the temple that has the greatest significance. It shows that man is no longer separated from God by our sin. Jesus has paid for sin and brought mankind to God.

1. **When have you been separated from a loved one? What was that like?**

Encourage people to share what it was like to be all alone. They may express how vulnerable that they felt or wondered what they had done that others had abandoned them. The point is to help us understand the separation that Jesus felt on the cross.

2. **What happened from the sixth to the ninth hour (noon to 3 PM) (27:45) What mood do you think that created around the cross?**

Jesus had been nailed to the cross at the third hour (9 AM) and was mocked by bystanders during that time. At noon, darkness settled over the land for three hours. Along with the other events like the earthquake and the dead rising and walking through Jerusalem (27:51-53), this would seem to have been caused by God. It seemed that creation was testifying to the injustice of Jesus' death. The text never says what the mood of the bystanders was, but it would be surprising if people didn't fall silent as so many "spooky" things happened at once. Was the darkness a sign of God's judgment? (Amos 8:9)

3. **What does Jesus cry out at the ninth hour? (27:46) What do you think His words meant?**

Jesus cries out the first line of Psalm 22, "My God, My God, why have you forsaken me?" In the psalm, this is part of a prayer of expectation for deliverance and not only a cry of abandonment. God had to forsake His son because of our sins, but that forsaking always was put in the shadow of the resurrection and victory over sin.

4. **When have you felt like God has forgotten you? How are God's words in Hebrews 13:5-6 a comfort to you at those times?**

Most of us have felt like God has forgotten us. We may even feel that strongly when we have prayed for something for a long time and help didn't come. Let the group talk about those experiences and take a look at Hebrews 13:5-6. Here, God promises us that he

will never leave us or forsake us. When we know God is our helper,
we do not need to be afraid. Verse 5 is a quote from Deut. 31:6
where God gives this promise to encourage Joshua.

5. **What do the bystanders think Jesus shouted in verse
   47? How does one person try to help Jesus**?

Those near the cross thought that Jesus was calling for Elijah.
Some interpreted Malachi 4:5, "See, I will send you the prophet
Elijah" as a promise from God to send Elijah to rescue those who
were suffering. Thus, the people thought that Jesus was calling
Elijah to help Him. John records (John 19: 28-29) that one of them
lifted up a stick with sour wine after Jesus had said' "I thirst". The
help seems genuine and the liquid was probably present for the
soldiers to drink. Others continue to taunt Jesus and mock "His call
for Elijah" wanting to see if Elijah would actually come.

6. **With His lips now moist, Jesus cried out. Then what
   happened? (27:50) What does John's gospel (John
   19:30) say that Jesus spoke?**

Jesus cried out and died. The cry recorded here may be Jesus' words, "It is finished" (John 19:30). The cry was the climax of Jesus's time on the cross and showed that Jesus was conscious up to his death. That He gave up His Spirit shows that he was in total control. The cry was a proclamation to everyone present and to all of us that His death on the cross had accomplished its purpose.

7. **How would you explain why it was necessary for Jesus to die to a non-Christian? What do you think life would be like for you if Jesus hadn't died?**

Answers will vary, but this is an important question because Jesus wants all of us to share the cross with others. Any answer will need to share how all men sin and need salvation and how Jesus provided redemption on the cross when we could not save ourselves. Take time to let people begin to fashion their own witness to Jesus. Be sure to include the difference that Jesus makes in their lives for people will want to know what they gain by having Jesus. The second question may help them understand what Jesus brings to their lives and what He can bring to the lives of people around them.

8. **What happened in the temple at the moment that Jesus died? (27:51) What was the purpose of this curtain in the temple?**

The temple was in three sections. The courtyards were for the people. The holy place held the candles and showbread and only priests could serve there. Finally, the Most Holy Place was a place where God dwelt and only the high priest could enter once a year on the Day of Atonement. At the moment that Jesus died, the curtain between the holy place and the Most Holy Place was torn in two. This curtain separated the Holy God from His sinful people. Through Jesus' death, man was no longer separated from God because of his sin. Mankind could now approach God because of the forgiveness of the cross.

9. **What separates men from God today? How can we help others break down those walls?**

Answers will vary, but we often separate ourselves from God by our unbelief and pride. All sin can be forgiven, but many do not want to be forgiven or believe in a God that they cannot see or cannot control. It is important to see that our example and our witness can be used by the Holy Spirit to break down these walls and bring people to faith. We must be willing to share what we know about God and how He works in our lives so that people can see the truth about God and experience His love.

10. The centurion saw all that had happened and declared Jesus was the Son of God (27:54) What have you seen or experienced that convinces you that Jesus is God?

Answers will vary, but it is important for us to consider this question. Many of us have been Christians all our lives and have never known life outside of faith. There may be someone in your group who came to faith as an adult. Have them share why they believe this story and the power of the cross so that others can ponder why they believe the story of the cross so strongly. Most of us will be challenged at some point in our lives. If we know the answer to the question before hand, we can express our devotion to God when we are asked.

29 Darkness turns to Joy-Matt 28:1-10

Her daughter Jill had been in an accident on the way to school. The officer on the phone didn't know any more than that the car was totaled, and Jill was taken to Memorial Hospital. As Mary drove to the hospital, she cried and prayed and hoped that her daughter was still alive. She ran into the hospital and was taken to an emergency room where they were putting a cast on Jill's left arm. She was alive with a broken arm and a few bruised ribs. Embracing her daughter, Mary cried and never wanted to let go. The darkness had turned to joy. Thank you, Lord, for another miracle!

Early Easter morning, the women who had remained at the cross (Matt. 27:55-56) came bringing spices to finish the burial of Jesus. They had no thought of the resurrection and were not even sure how they would move the stone blocking the tomb's entrance (Mark 16:3). Yet their darkness would soon turn to joy. The story of Easter is the light in the life of every Christian. It separates those who only know about Jesus from those who believe in Him. It is the center of the Christian faith and the touchpoint of God's love for us.

1. **What was the saddest day you ever experienced? Who was there with you?**

Each person will have their own story. Some will know immediately what day that would have been. It might have been a death of someone dear to them or being fired from a job. Others may not have a specific day. The point of this question is to empathize with the women in the story.

2. **Who visits the tomb? (28:1) Why and when did they come?**

Mary Magdalene and the other Mary came at dawn. Both of them had been at the cross (Matt. 27:56) and followed Joseph so that they would know where the tomb was located (Matt. 27:61). The women came early in the morning after the Sabbath because they had not had any time to prepare the body before the Sabbath began at sunset on Friday (Mark 16:1)

3. **What emotions do you think the women had that morning as they walked to the tomb?**

Have the group put themselves in the place of the women. The women came to the tomb to finish the job of embalming a friend that they were sure was dead. Normal answers might include crying,

shock, and a sense of helplessness or loss. It would be the feeling

that one of us might have visiting a grave a day or two after the

burial of a close relative or friend in order to place flowers on the

grave.

4. What events had happened at the tomb before the women had come that morning? (28:2-4)

The Lord had prepared the tomb for the visitors by a violent

earthquake and a visit by an angel which scared the guards so that

the women had an unimpeded visit at the tomb. The description of

the angel provides ample reason for the guards to be afraid. The

angel also rolled the stone away so that the women could see into

the tomb and be witnesses to Jesus' resurrection. God knew that a

closed tomb guarded by soldiers would not have allowed the women

to see that Jesus was gone or hear the witness of the angel.

5. What news did the angel tell the women? (28:5)

The angel reassures the women that they have no reason to fear.

They are looking for Jesus, but He is risen. The angel reminds the

women that Jesus had told them three times (Matt. 16:21, 17:22-23,

and 20:17-19) that He would rise. They should not have been

surprised because Jesus had prepared them for this moment. Each of the three predictions in Matthew's gospel gives more details than the prediction before it. The angel also invites the women to look into the tomb and see the place where Jesus had been laid. John's gospel (John 20:6-7) even describes the grave clothes to show that no one could have made off with the body.

6. **How did you come to know that Jesus had arisen? What convinced you that the account of His resurrection was true?**

Many of us have been Christians since our childhood and thus have just accepted the resurrection as truth. Others in the group may have come to faith as an adult. Let the group share why they believe in the resurrection. Some may believe because of a miracle that happened in their lives. Others may believe because the story has convinced them. Some may not be sure why they believe. Accept that and let the group discuss what convinces people that Jesus is alive so that they can share that witness with others.

7. **What command did the angel give the women (28:7) which Jesus repeats to them (28:10)?**

The angel commands the women to proclaim what they have seen to the disciples in verse 7. Jesus will repeat this command in verse

10. Remember that the disciples were gathered together (Luke

24:9) and were probably experiencing the same fear and sadness

that the women had felt as they went to the tomb. God's concern for

His servants is evident. He wants the disciples to have the good

news as soon as possible. Sadly, the men did not believe the

women's testimony (Luke 24:11) because the resurrection of Jesus

seemed like nonsense.

8. **Who is Jesus telling you to go and tell the news of the empty tomb?**

Answers will vary, but have the group think about people that they

know who are struggling or who have questions about life. God

gives us all opportunities to let the message of the gospel help the

hurting around us. Many are satisfied in life and are not open to the

message. Each person should make a list of the hurting who the

Holy Spirit can prepare to listen and believe our message.

9. **How does Jesus show love for the women and His disciples (28:9-10)**

Jesus could have just let the angel present the message, but in His

love for them, He appeared directly to them as they hurried away from the tomb. His words assure them that He harbors no anger to them or to the disciples who He calls "brothers". His greeting is one of closeness and love for them. He also gives instructions for the disciples to go to Galilee even though He will see them in Jerusalem later that day (Luke 24:36). The disciples who deserted Jesus in the Garden of Gethsemane and at the cross are forgiven and restored. Jesus will not desert them.

10. How do the words of Jesus comfort and challenge you? What stands out to you in this account of the resurrection?

Answers will vary and may include the lengths that God went to in order that people might know that Jesus rose or the love of Jesus shown to the women and disciples who did not believe in Him at first. I think of the joy that they had that day of actually seeing Jesus and the women's reaction of falling at His feet and worshipping Him (as God?).

32 Disappointed with Easter? - Luke 24: 13-32

Janna hated going to church and Sunday school. The songs were old. She didn't know her Bible well enough to understand the pastor's sermons. All she knew was that church was about being good and helping people she didn't know. The only thing good about it was that Dad took them out for brunch after Sunday school. Then one Sunday, the service and Sunday school were led by a missionary from Africa. He started with a few Old Testament passages and opened up the Easter story as a story of joy. Christ was changing lives for those who knew Him. He finished the message by showing pictures of children like her smiling and digging a well so the village. Janna wanted that happiness and began searching the scripture and praying for it from that day. Now, living with Jesus has become her joy.

Two men were walking from Jerusalem to Emmaus, a village seven miles away, on the afternoon or early evening of Easter. The men heard accounts that Jesus was alive but did not believe them. They were discouraged and disappointed as they discussed the events of Good Friday. They had high hopes for Jesus but found themselves frustrated that He had not been the

Messiah that they sought. Many today have rejected Jesus because they have the wrong picture of Jesus. Jesus joins in the discussion and helps all of us understand who the Messiah really is.

1. **What dreams of yours have been broken? Who did you talk with about your broken dreams?**

Answers will vary, but some in the group will talk about jobs that they didn't get or not being able to take the dream vacation. Others may share dreams like having children or finishing college that goes deeper and has longer effects. The point of this question is relate to the men on the road to Emmaus who had shattered dreams and to think about who they would share with if the situation arose in the future.

2. **On Easter, two men are walking to Emmaus. How long is the trip to Emmaus and what do they talk about? (24:13-14)**

Luke is the only gospel that tells the story of these two disciples who walked from Jerusalem on a seven mile trip to the town of Emmaus. The two men focused on their disappointments and did not think to stay and support the other disciples in Jerusalem. They may have been in Jerusalem during Good Friday and certainly were present on Easter morning (24:22). Puzzled about the meaning of what they had heard they rehash the stories to try and understand what has happened.

3. How have the trials and disappointments of life and ministry affected you?

Answers will vary, but the discussion can be an opportunity to talk about the struggles and disappointments that we all had in ministry and in life. Don't let the conversation on this question go on for too long. It is just a chance to admit that we all have frustrations like the two men did.

4. What question does Jesus ask the two men? (24:17) How do the men describe the events of the last couple days and their hopes for the ministry of Jesus? (24:19-24)

Jesus asks a simple question, "What things?" which unleashes a great teaching opportunity. The men have a chance to tell the facts which they assume that anyone who had been in Jerusalem would have known. Their discourse also expresses their dashed hopes and disappointments. Despite the women's witness and the prophecy of the resurrection from Jesus (Matt. 20:17-19), the two, like the disciples, had not put together the meaning of the events they had witnessed.

5. **What do you expect from the Christian life? How have you dealt with the times when you felt disappointed with God or with your life?**

Answers will vary, but many of us believe that everything will always turn out well just because we are Christians. The Christian life is not a guarantee that we will never have trouble. Our joy is that we have a savior and friend who will help us through the troubles that come in life. We are not exempt from trouble but can conquer problems with His help and character.

6. **How does Jesus respond to the two men? (24:25) What does Jesus need to explain before He can reveal Himself to them? (24:26-27)**

Jesus calls the men fools because they were so caught up in the Jewish picture of the Messiah as a conquering king that they could not see the simple truth of the Old Testament scriptures. I picture Jesus starting with the promise of a savior (Gen. 3:15) and other prophecies in the Pentateuch and working through sections talking about the suffering servant passages like Isaiah 53 and the one who is forsaken in Psalm 22. Jesus wanted these two and all of us to look at all of the scripture, not just the pictures of Messianic glory like Psalm 2. If they were going to understand who He was when they saw Him in glory, they had to understand why He died as their Savior.

7. **How well could you explain Jesus' death and resurrection to another person? What connection is there between our lack of understanding and a lack of faith in hard times?**

Like the two disciples, we often do not know as much as we think about the story and meaning of the cross and Easter resurrection. This exercise helps us to see how much or how little we know so that we can continue to learn more about Jesus and His gift of salvation for us. Like the two disciples, we will find ourselves discouraged more often if we know the message of the Bible and the person of Jesus only vaguely. Those who have grown in the faith and who have studied the Bible will have a much easier time of sharing God's Word and message of salvation. You have to grow in order to give.

8. **When were the men allowed to see Jesus' true nature? (24:30-31) How had Jesus' teaching prepared them for this moment? (24:32)**

Having asked Jesus to stay so that they might learn more from Him, the two saw Jesus in a simple act of fellowship. The lesson was over and the Holy Spirit had prepared their hearts through the teaching that Jesus had done. In the breaking of the bread, their eyes were opened so that they could see the confirmation of all that they had heard about in scripture. Jesus' teaching had burned inside them and opened the eyes of their heart so that they could see the savior right before them.

9. **When in your life have you come closest to giving up on ministry or on faith in God? What opened your eyes and strengthened your faith?**

Answers will vary. As a pastor, I find that I am discouraged when people reject the gospel message or when a project has not gone well. Let the class discuss their own times of weak faith. Let them also discuss how God helped them through those times. God often lifts me up through a time of prayer, a special devotion or Bible study or just the words of a friend. God has many ways that He uses to bring the message of scripture to us and encourage us with the gospel.

10. Why are we often "slow of heart to believe" (24:25)?

What do you think Jesus would say to you and to your

group if He walked down the road with you?

The point of this question is that any of us could have behaved just

like the two disciples in the text. We all have times where we give in

to our culture or are disappointed when events don't go the way that

we wanted them to go. Jesus will open the scriptures to us if we let

Him. I have often pictured Him telling me the words of John 14:1,

"Do not let your hearts be troubled. Trust in God; trust also in me."

Those are words that He spoke to his discouraged disciples the

night before He died and they are word confirmed by His

resurrection. He wants us to trust that there is nothing He cannot

handle in our lives.

Events of the heart of the Passion

Thursday	
Preparation for the Passover	Matt. 26:17-19
The Last Supper	Matt. 26:20-29
Upper Room teaching	John 14-16
High Priestly Prayer	John 17
Gethsemane	Matt 26:36-46
Betrayal and Arrest	Matt. 26:47-56
Jewish trials and Peter	Matt. 26:57-75
Friday	
Judas hangs himself	Matt. 27:3-10
First trial before Pilate	Luke 23:1-7
Trial with Herod	Luke 23:8-12
Second trial before Pilate	Luke 23:13-25
Trip to Golgotha	Luke 23:26-31
Crucifixion	Matt. 27:33-56
Burial	John 19:38-42
Easter Sunday	

The resurrection	Matt. 28:1-10
Mary Magdalene sees Jesus	John 20:10-18
The road to Emmaus	Luke 24:13-32
Appearance to the disciples	John 20:19-31

About the author

Rev. Mark Etter has been a pastor for over thirty years and is currently the pastor of Bethany Lutheran Church in Erlanger, KY. Rev. Etter has published several books of Adult Bible studies and numerous devotions and youth studies with Concordia Publishing House in St. Louis. He is a certified pastoral coach for Coach Advance of Cleveland, OH and has served in several capacities like LWML counselor, evangelism chairman, and circuit counselor for the larger church. He and his wife, Joan, have three grown children.

The Bible has been the key to all the joys in his life as it has affected his marriage, his health and his character. He hopes that these studies help people to draw closer to Christ and apply the wisdom of the scripture to their lives. These are devotions with depth to change your destiny. My prayer is that you use this book as a tool to grow in your own faith and then use the Bible studies to share God's wisdom by leading others through the Bible studies. To God be the glory for any insights that are new to you in this book. I pray that this book and the others in the series are a blessing to you. If you want other devotions, I put material up on my website weekly at www.32daysdevotions. May the Lord bless you all.

Other titles from Higher Ground Books & Media:

Wise Up to Rise Up by Rebecca Benston

A Path to Shalom by Steen Burke

Overcomer by Forrest Henslee

Miracles: I Love Them by Forest Godin

32 Days with Christ's Passion by Mark Etter

Knowing Affliction and Doing Recovery by John Baldasare

Out of Darkness by Stephen Bowman

I Don't Want to Be Like You by Maryanne Christiano-Mistretta

For His Eyes Only by John Salmon, Ph.D

The Magic Egg by Linda Phillipson

The Tin Can Gang by Chuck David

Whobert the Owl by Mya C. Benston

Add these titles to your collection today!

http://highergroundbooksandmedia.com

www.ingramcontent.com/pod-product-compliance
Lightning Source LLC
LaVergne TN
LVHW011343080426
835511LV00005B/112